T0374231

THE
SPIRIT
OF
GOD

THE HEART OF MANKIND

TIMOTHY J. BROWN

THE SPIRIT OF GOD
THE HEART OF MANKIND

iUniverse books may be ordered through booksellers or by contacting:

iUniverse
1663 Liberty Drive
Bloomington, IN 47403
www.iuniverse.com
844-349-9409

ISBN: 978-1-6632-5965-3 (sc)
ISBN: 978-1-6632-5966-0 (e)

Library of Congress Control Number: 2024900525

Print information available on the last page.

iUniverse rev. date: 02/27/2024

DEDICATION

I want to dedicate this book to my loving wife, Jaime. She supported me on a daily basis. She encouraged me when I was having a hard time writing. She read through the pages as often as I asked. She listened to me rant and rave. She has been here for me all the way through writing this book. She truly loves me as much as any man could think or ask. I never thought I would ever find a woman as true to me as she is. I'm looking forward to spending the rest of my happy life with her. I love you, Jaime.

I also want to dedicate this book to Victoria and Steven, the most wonderful children a person could ever have in life. I love them both with my life. I am also dedicating this book to all who read it. Thank you.

PREACH THE WORD!

CONTENTS

ACKNOWLEDGMENT

I would like to say that many people have influenced my life. My grandfather just the way he prayed in church you knew God was listening. I wanted to pray as he did. My Aunt, she would read from the Bible and tell stories of her experiences with the LORD. My brother's love for the LORD has been an inspiration over the years. My Pastor, he was like a father to me over the years. Dr. Jim Richards has been a great mentor. I have read and studied his books, which I have pulled from in this book. These include *Grace: The Power to Change* and *The Gospel of Peace.*

1

BEGINNING THE JOURNEY

THE REASON I AM WRITING THIS BOOK IS FOR UNDERSTANDING THE Spirit of God. I've been a believer for forty-three years. In these forty-three years, I've found a lot of things that cloud our relationships with God. I have found that we really don't understand the Spirit of God. In all the years on this journey, I have been far from perfect in finding my way. It has been difficult dealing with all the challenges. God has taught me how to walk through those challenges. We humans are difficult to understand for many different reasons. I know that is a vague statement. I don't understand why anyone would not want to enjoy the life of God. God means for us to enjoy life. In fact, he has gone to a lot of trouble to make sure of it. People's doctrines make seeing what he has done difficult. It has been very difficult to work and find my way through the doctrines of people. The things written here are proven facts straight from the scriptures and not opinions. I have spent my life studying and meditating on the scriptures. Having said that, what do I mean? This has led me to become a biblical scholar. What is a biblical scholar? A biblical scholar may work in isolation, writing and researching. A biblical scholar may also be different from a theologian. A theologian works to put together a comprehensive system of doctrine, whereas a Bible scholar may be content simply to clarify what the Bible says without trying to systematize it. In all my research and studies, I have found many things that are incorrect or misrepresented. Doctrines sometimes take away from the true meaning of what God is trying to say to us. I have spent my life finding the truth away from the doctrines of people. The word *doctrine* means teachings that have been organized to support a belief system. That does not mean that doctrines are all wrong. Paul said that doctrines are okay but need to be Bible doctrines. Bible doctrines should be backed up by the whole of the scriptures. We should not take scripture out of context to make the Bible say what we like it to say. Paul told Timothy the spirit says expressly that, in the latter times, people will depart from the faith and teach doctrines of evil thinking (1 Timothy 4:1). He also told him that they would pull to themselves teachers who would teach what they wanted to hear rather than teach the words of life (2 Timothy 4:3).

I want to spend a little bit of time talking about belief systems. A belief system means a set of principles or tenets that together form the basis of a religion, philosophy, or moral code. A person's or society's belief system is a set of beliefs about what is right and wrong and what is true and false.

I would like to say that not all belief systems are wrong. However, considering the truth of scripture and salvation, we need to get this right. In a belief system, we can believe whatever we want. The problem is that if we want the true benefit of God's word, we need to believe correctly. The book of Proverbs says that, as a person believes in his or her heart, so he or she is. In other words, we live our lives from our belief systems because of what we believe.

This can be very unhealthy if we do not work from the blueprint from which we were created. God created humans and gave them an instruction manual. It is just like a blueprint; when you begin to build something, you have to follow the blueprint. If you do not, you will end up with a lot of problems. It is the same with the blueprint our creator has given to us. If we do not follow it, we will not only have issues with ourselves but cause problems for others as well.

Let us look at the Ten Commandments for just a moment. The first two are for honoring God, but the last eight are for the protection of humankind. It doesn't take much to see how not following our blueprint is causing chaos in every corner of the globe. This is very sad when God's plan was for us to have abundantly full lives with peace and rest.

He has given us everything we need for abundant, full lives. We either don't believe this, don't know it, or haven't experienced it in one form or another. That is why I am writing this book. We all should want to invest in ourselves for the betterment of our lives. Jesus said he came to give us life it to its fullest. Peter said we have all things that pertain to life and godliness. Paul said to focus on a good report; whose report will we believe? I choose to believe the report of the Lord. Paul said we are troubled on every side, yet not distressed; we are perplexed, but not in despair; we are persecuted, but not forsaken; and we are cast down, but not destroyed. This shows that the abundant life is manifesting itself in our lives every day. God says to come and taste and see that he is good. In other words, by changing our belief systems to his belief system, we can prove he is good. Changing the way we believe is not easy, but it is possible. Jesus said with God, all things are possible. We have been justified by Jesus to fellowship with God on a daily basis or every second basis. We have the grace of God. Grace is the ability of God working from our hearts to enable us to live our lives the way God intended. The grandest thing to know is that God wants us to have good lives and experience them on a daily basis.

Not knowing God and not experiencing him the way he desires will leave us without the full benefits. This is why we should know all about the spirit of God. There is so very much we can experience. If we will decide to allow God to show us, we can understand him as he truly is.

I spent the better part of twenty years experiencing God the way he intended me to. I didn't understand faith righteousness, how his spirit works in us, grace as the ability of God, and also how much he loves me unconditionally because of Jesus. These things could take some time to explain. I will spend some time through the book explaining each of these things. I will say that God intends for us to do what he says in the scriptures. Whatever we spend time meditating on and thinking about will be how we live our lives.

Faith righteousness was one of the hardest things I had to figure out. Some people might wonder why that is. I was a very conservative believer. I did not understand how the scriptures could say to do what God says and be in right standing with God without doing anything. It is true we cannot experience the blessings of God without doing and meditating on the things he says. However, we have been given everything needed to have everything God promises. We can fellowship with God without doing everything right. This will bring us into line with God because we can fellowship with him. This is his intention. Continuing in the light and living in the light will bring you into life and the truth. We have a choice about whether to do what he says. We also have to understand dead works and living works. Dead works are those works that do not matter to God.

Dead works are like the Pharisees. There was a Pharisee and a sinner. The Pharisee thanked God that he was not like that sinner. He fasted twice a week and did other works. The sinner beat upon his chest and asked God to have mercy on him. Jesus said the sinner was the one who obtained mercy. Works that are alive come from fellowshipping with God and experiencing everything through faith in the love of God because of Jesus. Understanding the grace of God works through faith. Believing in the death, burial, and resurrection of Jesus from the heart empowers us to live out the life of God. The life of God is the zoe. The zoe of God is the God kind of life or the quality life from the one who gives it. God gives us the best quality of life we could have. He has given us a beautiful place to live and all the things to with which to enjoy life. It is hard to believe that because of the evil world all around us, unless we understand that God loves us and wants us to be successful. We can't experience the things we are talking about unless we look with soft and repentant hearts that want the things God has to offer. I have so much faith in what I am saying because I have lived it and walked it out. The experience of living it out is the way we prove it is true. It really works and it works just like God says it will. I have so many stories to tell in this journey that I have been on.

God gave me a dream when I was living in an apartment wanting to move into a house and have a yard for my children to play in. We wanted the house with the little picket fence and a dog. We did not get the little picket fence but we got the dog, the yard, and a brick house. It was a year's journey that I walked through. In the dream, I saw God give us a brick house to live in. I found a brick house that was for sale for twenty-five thousand dollars. The house needed some work, but I knew I had the skill to make it a really nice home. I didn't have the money to buy the house, but I knew an investor. I told him what I had found and asked him to finance it for me. In exchange, I would lease the house to own. He had done this for other people I knew. He bought the house and kept it for himself. I thought, *There is no way this is right. God had shown me the house in a dream. I knew he had.* I was devastated in the worst way. I totally misunderstood God, but it took me a while to understand that.

God has a way of wanting us to do things the right way so they will last a lifetime. He had a house, but my credit was bad because of some bad decisions and unpaid debts. God wanted me to have a fresh start. The house I found was being prepared for me for a year. It was a rental house that the owner was remodeling with a nice yard and a garden spot. It was right across the road from the apartments being remodeled. I went by there one day and saw a rental sign. I called the owner and rented the house. The owner asked if she could ask me a question. I said sure. She said, "I had the house for rent for a year. I advertised it everywhere but did not receive a response. After a year, I decided to put a for rent sign out. The very day I did, you called me before I returned home."

I said, "Well, God was getting my heart ready for a year and your heart ready for me. You made it look new, just like God had shown me in a dream. Then my heart was ready to do things right and I saw the sign and here we are." God does things just right. I would have skipped over doing all the right things not having learned the lessons needed for my future. One story goes right into another. I was handed a house that I bought after living in a rented house for six years. The lessons I learned have never left me. What I learned is how to apply the principles of God to my life. These principles were about prosperity and sowing and reaping. I am not talking about naming it and claiming it. I am talking about paying your debts, saving money, and building credibility.

Faithfulness was the biggest part of this whole thing. How does faithfulness play a part? You continue to do the right thing even when it looks like there is no end in sight. All things can look as if they are against you and you continue to be faithful. Jesus said if we continue in his word, we will be his disciples. In other words, Jesus was saying as you experience his word, you will learn to be faithful. Being faithful is the key factor in all that we learn with Yahweh. He says he is faithful even when we are not, and he is content to be so. Jesus also says if you're faithful over another person's things, he will give us our own. He says if we are faithful over little, he would make us rulers over much. I have seen this prove itself repeatedly. God is faithful.

God has never let me down, but I have not done what I should have much of the time. I have worked against God a lot. I have blamed God for my choices and I have blamed others as well. I went to the same church for twenty or so years. In all that time, I fought against God and against people who were trying to help me on my journey. I didn't know I was doing that, but I was. I have always found my way to repentance. Being hard-hearted doesn't always work that way. It makes life very hard. You also hurt the people around you who don't need to be hurt. It will mess up their lives and cause them to get off track in their lives. One of the things that has hurt me the most is when I have hurt other people. Jesus said it is better for you to have a big rock tied around your neck and be thrown into the sea than to hurt those young in the Lord. As leaders, learning how to follow the spirit of the Lord is everything.

Following the spirit of the Lord saves trouble for you, the Lord, and everyone else. As I have learned, to follow the principles of God is to follow the spirit of God. Some of us believe that letting our emotions run wild is the spirit of the Lord. However, our emotions are running wild and that is it. God really does want us to have stability in our lives and for our families to experience that as well. This is why it is so important to understand how to follow the spirit of the Lord the way it is intended. When you see someone enjoying a stable life, you are seeing God at work. This is something you should never forget.

Hold onto rest in your mind and peace in your heart. When our minds are still and at rest, we can hear God very clearly. There is nothing more important to the Lord than having a still mind. Jesus said we should not let our hearts be troubled, weighted down, or overcharged. Being overcharged causes us to lose hope. Without hope, we become sick, meaning we grieve and become depressed.

When we are depressed, we can't function the way we should. In turn, we will also begin to blame God and other people for our problems. We stay in this cycle until we decide to stop, pick ourselves up, remember the truth, and move forward. As we do this, we recover. It is better we do not keep repeating this cycle. It damages our hearts and makes them hard. By no means do we need to deal with hard hearts. Guarding your heart is the best way. Proverbs says to guard your heart above all else or put boundaries around it to protect it. The reason for this is that what we let in our hearts molds them into who and what we are. This process affects even the very cells in our bodies. It affects our health in ways that could lead to death. Most of the sickness we have is because of what is going on in our hearts. Let us work hard to put up the right boundaries so that we can live our lives in rest and peace. God wants that for us in every part of our lives and in the lives of the people around us. God really does have a plan for our lives and we need to believe that. These are not our plans but his.

2

A SPIRITUAL PERSON
JUDGES ALL THINGS

WHAT DOES IT MEAN THAT A SPIRITUAL PERSON JUDGES ALL THINGS? There are many things I could say. First, let us talk about what is spiritual. Spiritual is a mental disposition. It is a way of thinking—a way of thinking as God thinks. I want to make sure you understand. Before God destroyed the earth with water, he said, "My spirit will not always strive with man" (Genesis 6:3). The meaning for spirit here is perceive or understand, also to resemble a rational being. The Spirit is working in people to bring understanding about choosing God's ways.[1] The words "strive with man" mean to judge things or work through them using the judgment of God.[2] We should act from or live our lives by his principles. When God was passing judgment on humankind, he said that every imagination of the thoughts of his heart was evil continually.

This is something I have studied and researched for many years. Can you imagine? The heart is the very essence of who a human is. The essence of the heart even reaches into the cells, the building blocks of life. The heart is who we really are and how we live our lives. That is why we should renew our minds on a daily basis. In other words, we should

---

[1] H.W.F. Gesenius, *Hebrew and Chaldee Lexicon to the Old Testament Scriptures* (Grand Rapids, MI: Baker Publishing Group, 1979), 760–761.

[2] Gesenius, 197.

change the way we think. I know that sounds easy, but it is not easy at all. It takes a lifetime of work to realize we cannot achieve anything without God's help. We don't want to create a burden that Jesus already removed. We do need to take responsibility to recognize that renewing the mind will take a lifelong journey to complete.

I know it has taken my whole life to change the way I think and believe. When I first started my journey, it felt like I was going to die from the grief I experienced. In reality, that is exactly what was happening. I was, and am, dying daily to selfishness and self-centeredness. When I was changing my belief system, it was so very difficult to walk through. I found all I had believed for my entire life was wrong. That is a lot to deal with and walk through. I wanted the truth, and what I thought was the truth was not. When you have spent your whole life believing something, it is very hard to change that belief. Remember what I said about it taking a lifetime? Well, it does. I kept thinking I had, then I would learn something else and would have to go through another change. Most of us will live our lives not knowing the real truth about life. We may never put forth the effort to look into the real meaning of life and how things are supposed to be. We just allow life to make us hard-hearted and we find ourselves in traps. We never become too old to change; it is just harder if we wait. Do you know how we say he is just set in his ways? He is in a mindset; we will talk more about this later. It is also harder if we don't have anything to work with at all in us. No one taught us while we were reaching the age where things are set in stone. We think about the seed sower in the scriptures. We really do not realize how important it is to teach our children the scriptures. Did you know that children develop their sets of beliefs between the ages of three and seven?[3]

---

[3] Beth Kobliner, "Money habits are set by age 7. Teach your kids the value of a dollar now," PBS News Hour, posted April 5, 2018, https://www.pbs.org/newshour/economy/making-sense/money-habits-are-set-by-age-7-teach-your-kids-the-value-of-a-dollar-now.

If we do not teach them early, they will not have anything to work with. When we don't have anything in us to work with, it is almost impossible to make the change. When I was just a little boy, my aunt taught my siblings and me about God. My grandparents always made me go to church, so I had that influence growing up. I had something to work with when I started to follow the Lord.

It is hard enough with influence in our lives. Without it, even God says it is almost impossible to make a change. That is not to say we are without hope. We are never without hope as long as we are alive. Jesus paid for our sins so we could have many things and time is one of them. The important thing is slowing down your mind and putting the care of things on the Lord because he has already taken care of them. We just don't need to pick them up. When we don't have anything to work with, in other words we don't have the word in us. The scripture says the word of God is alive and powerful, and it discerns the thoughts and intentions of the heart. It shows you what is really going on inside your thinking processes. It is important for us to understand the intent of the heart. When someone asks about your intentions with his or her daughter or friend, he or she wants to know what you have in mind for that person. The word works like this all the time. What are your intentions about anything? This is about judging as a spiritual person all things that are inside of you. It also means judging with the things that are inside you, such as the spirit of God in you, leading you down that path of life.

We really have no idea how important we are to our Father. He has the best intentions in everything for us. The problem is we don't believe that. In turn, we don't act from the standpoint that God loves us and wants the best for us. We need to know him from that view and opinion. Hope is a confident expectation of good. When we have that confident expectation of good, we have hope. Hope, when put off, causes the heart to become sick. In other words, it causes the heart to grieve and can lead to depression. Depression leads to many bad decisions, such as using things that seem to take the pain away. The scriptures says when we cast off our restraints, we lose our vision and perish. The fact is we stop experiencing death inside. When we don't have a vision for our future, we lose hope or have grief and depression. Hope is a present and a future thing that we need to keep ourselves healthy. Without it, we crash, burn, and don't reach our goals.

Some people may ask why we need goals. Why can't we live from day to day and never plan? We just talked about this and what it causes. How does anyone know what he or she wants for the future? I think everyone wants a good outcome for the future. We can start making decisions that will cause good results for that end. We should never be afraid of small beginnings; we have to start somewhere. How do we know that God has good intentions for us? Sometimes it seems he wants to take away all the good stuff. It is perfectly fine to wonder or have that question. God says come and try me out and see what my intentions are for you. All decisions are judgments, and this is how a spiritual person judges all things. As we make decisions, we learn to trust.

People think we are supposed to trust God blindly. There is nothing further from the truth. Faith or trust is never blind. As a matter of a fact, God said to build faith or trust over a period of time. Trust is not given; it is earned and that takes time. If you make friends with an angry person, you will become an angry person. If you want to be a millionaire, don't ask someone who is not; ask a millionaire. Ask the person, "How did you become a millionaire?" It is the same with God. Don't we want to know why he says don't kill, or desire your friend's wife, or look at your neighbor's things and want what he or she has? These things prove to me we can trust God because they offer protection for us and others.

We often make things so difficult. We must know the whys and why nots. God teaches us that we should supplement our faith with humility, diligence, kindness, temperance, patience, love, and chastity. We should also have knowledge, self-control, and steadfastness. Above all is the God kind of love. Love is the keeping factor and the foundation that all things should produce. Without love, it is all dead. This is called dead works. Dead works do not produce the life of God within us. What is the life of God? It is the quality of life that God gives. The quality of life that God gives is joy, peace, hope, mercy, prosperity, wholeness, fulfillment, deliverance, friendships, and perfection. Without knowing that God has given us these things without any real effort of our own makes it a constant struggle that is impossible to achieve (2 Peter 1:3). These things are here for us to walk out.

This gives us such peace of mind and causes life to be wonderful and fulfilling in every aspect on a daily basis. This seems so hard to believe in the world around us. That is why the scripture says the natural mind receives not the things of God.

It is amazing how we move and live and have our being by the Lord. What does that mean, you might say? It means a lot! Everything we would ever need when God made us was given to us by his spirit. Earlier I mentioned that when God made the man, he breathed into him and put his spirit inside the man. His spirit lived in the man until the man totally rejected it. Then came the time before the flood and God said his spirit would not continue to be desired within humans. Being without the wisdom of God working with you in all you do is dangerous. We should allow ourselves to practice the judgments of God. Our judgments keep us from the wisdom of God. We have such a privilege in our lives to live our lives making judgments as God would. The scriptures back this up in every way. Meditation is the key. Meditation is not about humming. It involves seeing the picture in our minds, as real and active in the way we live our lives. You can meditate any time. Sometimes we think of it as dreaming or daydreaming. When I was working in construction, I had a lot of time to be thinking/meditating about God's judgments. I loved it because that is when I received a lot of my understanding of the scriptures.

There is no formula we all have to learn our to have fellowship with God. Fellowship is a way to walk in our daily lives. A lot of time, we don't understand how important this is. There is only one truth but many ways to find our ways to it. This is because we are evil looking at truth through a glass darkly. Many times, we believe there are many truths or many ways to God. This is a human making a way for himself or herself with his or her evil heart. Thank God for his love and mercy, Thank God for Jesus; if it were not for him, we would have no chance. God is on our side but not making excuses for us in Jesus. This can be very confusing, but it shouldn't be.

A man came up to me one day after a speaking event. He said, "I love what you said today." The thing is I didn't say anything at all like that. He was seeing things from his perspective, through his belief system, and the way he had trained himself to see things. This is fine; we don't all get there the same way. We don't need to make excuses for ourselves and lie against the truth. It's funny how we are forgiven and still have bad things inside of us. There is a difference between being forgiven and walking something out and experiencing the fruit. It's one thing to plant a seed in the ground and then take fruit from the tree. There is a process to this. We have the fruit given to us in the seed, but the tree must grow into the fruit. The knowledge of the fruit, the tree, and the way they grow is in the seed.

Have you ever seen a tree straining to make fruit? No, we haven't. Wouldn't it be funny to walk by a tree and see it push out apples? I think it would be strange, to say the least. Grace works the same way. We sometimes believe that grace is the unmerited favor, and it is, but it is so much more. Grace is God's ability that works from the heart to enable us to produce fruit. Because of his spirit in us, we have this ability. This is what this book is all about. My goal for this book is for us to understand how all this works. There is so much that has been turned and twisted because our hearts are crooked in the way we understand the things of God.

I have spent my whole life working through my crooked heart's way of thinking. I know how difficult it is to let God mold us. We want to work from the understanding we have, and understand God's ways and principles because it seems right. There is a way that seems right to us, but it is the way of death. Death comes before we die and it becomes permanent after we die. What do I mean by this? The scriptures say there is life and death in the power of our speech. What we meditate on is what comes back to us in actions. What we say out loud is what comes from the abundance of what we meditate on. This works in a constant cycle. We have to break that cycle. We think things work on a linear cycle but they work in a circular cycle. It always comes back around so we fully reap the consequences. We call it karma or reaping what we sow.

We believe a lot of the time that God is out to get us if we sin. However, it is what we sow that gets us. When we don't see immediate results, we don't think we will ever reap them and continue to do the same thing. When we begin to see the results, we ask why this is happening to us. We ask why God doesn't love us or why he is doing this to us. The harvest of our sowing is coming back to us. We want it to go away, but just as it took time to sow, it takes time to turn it around. Sometimes, this seems very hard to do. It is possible. Remember to continue to sow proper seeds until you see the results you should be seeing. We need to get away from people who think the wrong way and be around people who teach and live the right way. Remember, what a person thinks inside himself or herself is what he or she becomes. Think of it this way: if you want to prosper, don't set yourself around people who live from paycheck to paycheck.

I hope we are beginning to understand how to reach our goals as we move through these chapters and read from the scriptures. We will see how to get there and begin to experience the results we are looking for without effort. I love the no effort principle. That is grace working, and grace is the power we need to make it all happen.

Please don't skip around in this book. You will not obtain proper results and apply what you are learning to your daily lives. This is important. There are no formulas, but we must apply the ways of God in order for there to be change. We have learned a lot, I believe, and I also believe we are ready to see those results. Pressure only brings grief into our lives because of failure. This takes our hope and goals away. Without goals, we will not make it to the place we desire. Our desires come from God as we get to know him and think and act as he does. Remember this: he wants us to prove his ways to be the truth by living and experiencing them on a daily basis. Doing so produces character and character produces hope. Seeing those results brings life instead of death or a life without hope. Keep reading and enjoy the results. Life is better than death. That is what we are doing here. It is a great thing to invest in ourselves when we know the good it brings.

3

TALKING ABOUT THE KINGDOM

DID YOU KNOW THAT JESUS IS KING OVER ALL THE EARTH? HE SITS AT God's right hand and is ruling the nations right now. You might say he is not doing a great job. Oh, he is; we just don't understand how he rules the nations. This is not what I want to write about in this book. This is another book that I am working on.

This book is about how the spirit of God works inside of us on a daily basis. It is about how we follow him, how we talk to him, and how we use his judgments to govern our lives. The scripture says the kingdom is not where we can see it. The kingdom works inside of us. We have been talking about this for some time, and we will continue to talk about it so we can come to an understanding.

Knowing how the *government of God* works in us on the earth is vital to understanding how the spirit of God works in us and through us. Remember, Matthew 6:20 says, "Your kingdom come, your will be done in earth as it is in Heaven." This is what we are after to see this through. God has always wanted a kingdom of priests, a holy people who would lead the world to him. Peter says we are "living stones built up as a spiritual house for a holy priesthood." We are to offer up "spiritual sacrifices" (1 Peter 2:5).

Let us not get too far ahead of ourselves. We have much to discuss. I would like to talk a little about my history. When it comes to the

17

understanding of the *kingdom of God,* I have a long life story. I spent my life looking into the kingdom of God. I have never been the person who accepts what someone says about anything having to do with the scriptures.

Let us get started with my story. I grew up in church and was taught about God from the time I was in my baby bed. I know that sounds a little bit strange, but it is true. I remember seeing the Six-Day War that Israel fought with the twelve Arab nations and won. I remember my mother asking my dad why Israel was God's chosen people. He told her about this as I listened. I even remember the Wailing Wall in Jerusalem. Soldiers and Jewish leaders prayed and thanked God at the Wailing Wall. This was for their victory and for God's help. I knew as a young boy that I was to follow God, but did not understand how that was going to work or anything about it. I remember when I came of age at twelve years old and was baptized. I went to my dad and told him I wanted to be baptized and follow the Lord. My dad was not very God-conscious, so he asked me why I wanted to do this. All that I could say was I knew it was time for me to follow the Lord.

Dad did not prevent me from doing this, so I went to the church with all my family and was baptized. I didn't really start following the Lord at this point. I had many struggles within myself that I did not understand. I continued to live my life as a good person looking to the Lord and wanting to understand him. When I was eighteen, I smoked marijuana and had a very bad experience. I thought I was going to lose my mind. I prayed to God to heal my mind and I would follow him. My mind was healed but I did not follow him for another year. I waited until I was nineteen years old. In fact, I said because I was of legal age to buy alcohol, I would have a party and then follow the Lord. That is exactly what I did. On Sunday morning, I got up and went to church. I was so dedicated to the Lord at this point. When I came home that afternoon, I looked at the

Bible laying on the table and decided to read it through. I didn't stop until I had achieved this very thing. Then I started learning how to study the scriptures. I picked up several tools. I went on to attend several different types of churches. I began to see how there were different belief systems in every type of church. I only saw that they all had one common belief. They all agreed that the only way to salvation was through Jesus. They had common differences about how to get there.

This I labored many years to understand. This was a very hard road to travel. My family wanted me to follow their way, but their way was flawed to me. I had to find my own way down this path that seemed very wide and had many detours. Because of my struggles, I lost my way at times. I have always found my way back to the path. Because of these struggles, I found it harder to trust anyone to get me there. I really needed to have a mentor. I finally found one who was like a dad to me. I spent over twenty years listening to him. He taught me many things about living life as I observed him living his life. I came to a place where I knew I had to find my way without him and only follow God.

When I started on this path, I began to really study the scripture and prove the things I had known my whole life. When I say prove, I was already a scholar of the scriptures. I had enough knowledge of the scriptures and had memorized almost the entire Bible. Every night for fifteen years, I would listen to the scriptures as I was driving up and down the road. I memorized the book of Proverbs from three different translations. All of this was free from human-made doctrines. I am a counselor twice over from a world perspective and a biblical one. I have studied in psychology for many years in college, which helped a lot in understanding how the mind works. I also spent twenty years finding an understanding of the heart of people. All of this helped me understand how the spirit of God works in the believer and understand all about the kingdom on the earth.

First, we must understand the kingdom works in us; no one can see it working on the inside of us. We can see the fruits of its work in us. There are laws and principles that work in governing inside us. What are these laws and principles? They have outcomes that are positive and negative. God is the designer and maker of all things. This governing can work for us or against us. God is for us, but gives us a choice. The choice can cost us or benefit us in everything in life.

The first law is sowing and reaping. What is the law of sowing and reaping? I believe we have been taught about this so much our motives can be crooked. We have heard so much about sowing money into the kingdom and reaping money. This is mostly what we think about when it comes to sowing and reaping.

There is so much more to this than just money. Sowing and reaping works in everything in the kingdom. It is so exciting to be sharing this right now. I have spent my whole life figuring this stuff out. I am glad that I can share it with you here. God said he would write his laws on our hearts and in our minds. This book is all about how he does that. We have been given the right to choose the way we will live our lives, but God gives us the best options. He always has our best interests in mind and the best interests of others.

Sowing and reaping work this way. The scripture says life and death are in the power of the tongue. What does that mean? It is very practical. The more we get in agreement with what is being said out of our mouths, the more we begin to believe. When we plant a seed in the ground, it will need water and good soil to sprout. Once it sprouts, it needs water, nurturing, and the right amount of sunlight. The more we do this, the more it grows. It will finally bear fruit or come to maturity. Life for us works the same way in the kingdom. Jesus tells us to be careful how we hear and how we meditate on what we hear. The thoughts we give to what we hear will come back to us. The scripture says that as a person thinks in his or her heart, so he or she is. For example, someone may say something that potentially has the ability to hurt us. What the person says is not as important as how we allow it to hurt us. Taking hold of the hurt and making it ours is our choice. We know the old saying "sticks and stones may break my bones, but words will never hurt me." How we think (meditate) and choose to accept these words in our hearts gives them the potential to grow into hurt. Acceptance is everything, and a process of feelings and thoughts brings it to pass. We often do not realize we entertain thoughts that do not benefit the kingdom of God. We say we would never let a situation get to a certain point. Jesus said that if we look upon another person with lust, we have committed adultery in our hearts already. In other words, if the circumstances changed, we would do the deed. If we thought we would not be caught, we would follow through. No one would ever know. In the kingdom of God, God is looking at our hearts, wanting us to reap the good things we have sown. This is sowing and reaping.

There is also a law of faith. We think faith is for things and it can be. The law of faith has many ways of operation. There are all kinds of principles of faith. The principle of faith I would like to discuss is believing in the word of God or the principles of God. What is faith really? When you break it down, it is total trust in the Lord. Faith is not something we can see or something we follow blindly. Trust is something we gain over a period of time. Even God says this in the scriptures. You will find out about this in my references. In the meantime, it is all about fellowship with the Lord. As we fellowship with the Lord, our trust grows and develops with him. We will prove things as we live our lives fellowshipping with God. In relationships, we never know all there is to know about a person right away. It takes time to know the real person.

When I first started getting to know the Lord, I only knew what people had told me. They were not always correct because they heard what they knew from someone else. God is a good God, but when I started, I did not truly know that. I did not even know after I had spent many years in college. Just because we have a lot of knowledge does not mean we know God. We could only know about him. The law of faith only works through fellowship. This fellowship brings experience of God on a first-name basis. We can prove him out so that the law of faith can work from the heart.

Intimacy is the best word to describe this. When you think of intimacy, you think of synonyms: familiarity, affection, love, personal fellowship, and expression of first names. When you say each other's names during intercourse, it increases intimacy. I use this example because it brings understanding of the noun being explained. You may have noticed that I do not use the word *relationship* here. It is because the word *relationship* is not used in the scriptures; only *fellowship* is.

The word *fellowship* is derived from the Greek word *koinonia*. *Koinonia* can be defined as "holding something in common"[4] (1 John 1:3 and 6). It is specifically used fifteen times in the New Testament (e.g., Philippians 2:1–2, Acts 2:42, 1 John 1:6–7, and others). *Koinonia* describes the *unity of the spirit* that comes from Christians' shared beliefs, convictions, and behaviors. When those shared values are in place, genuine koinonia (biblical fellowship) occurs. This fellowship produces our mutual cooperation in God's worship, God's work, and God's will in the world. Because of the importance of Christian fellowship, it is essential to use biblical guidelines to govern our interactions with other professing believers.

I also wanted to say something here about the unity of the spirit. Agreement comes to mind. We sometimes take this very lightly. Jesus's statement about two or three gathering together means being in

---

[4] Joseph Thayer, *Thayer's Greek-English Lexicon of the New Testament* (Peabody, MA: Hendrickson Academic, 2023), G2842.

agreement with the father and with the truth of the scriptures. Whenever someone was accused of breaking the law, there had to be two or three creditable witnesses to bring the accusation. This was profoundly serious because someone's life was at stake. It is just as important when we gather together in his name.

The kingdom of God is also about faithfulness. The principal faithfulness is so vital in the kingdom of God. The scriptures say that if we are faithful, he will make us rulers over much. How does this work? I can use some great examples. I lived in my rental house before I bought my own home. I took better care of this person's house and property than I would have ever dreamed of taking care of my own. When I was ready to move, the landlord came to talk to me. She said in all her forty years of managing properties, she had never returned a deposit. She did not have to do any work to the house. We had taken such loving care of the property and made improvements, so it was ready to lease. She wanted to tell us personally what a faithful family we were. I believe in God's principles so much and demonstrated them so many times. How could I doubt him? He is such a wonderful father.

This makes me think of America. We have no idea how this country is fashioned after the principles of the father. Even if the church does not do its job, God has set things in order in this country. God is all about family and community. We are always complaining about paying taxes. We don't realize how taxes pay for our road systems, parks, sidewalks, landscaping in our cities, and so much more. This is all about faithfulness, which is a part of the kingdom of God. God has also made a way in this country for the helpless, the old, and the orphans through social security, food stamps, disability programs, and money. We don't realize how blessed we are.

God wants us to be responsible for the earth as well. He has established soil conversation programs that govern how we build and develop. We have people who govern trees, oceans, streams, rivers, lakes, and the animals. We do not realize how much the father is involved in all this. When we think of the kingdom of God, we should have these things in mind. God said he would write his laws in our hearts and in our minds as well. He says he will take out the hearts of stone and give us hearts of flesh. He says he will soften our hard hearts. This process is sometimes very rough, but it is a choice of life or death. Everyone has a journey, but there is only one path.

I want to stop here and talk about something. There are many ways to experience life and death. There is death when we die and are buried in the ground. God told Adam from the dust he came and unto dust he would return. Then there is death we experience when our connection to life is broken. That doesn't mean that every area of our connection is broken. The scriptures say that we should guard our hearts above all else for out of them come the boundaries of life. We can harden our hearts in areas where we don't listen to God and are shut off from experiencing zoe, the God kind of life. If and when we are walking in the word of God from the heart, it becomes alive in us. Jesus said if we continue in his word, we will know the truth and the truth will set us free. The word *know* here means to experience or gain access to the life of God.

4

THE LIFE OF GOD

WHAT IS THE LIFE OF GOD? IT IS A STATE OF BEING, IT IS THE BREATH of life, it is wisdom, and it is a choice. It is a way of life—the way we were created to live. Jesus said he came to give us life (zoe) and give it to us more abundantly or to its fullest experience. Peter said that we are given all things that pertain to life (zoe) and godliness. Peter also said he has granted to us his precious and great promises. Through them, we become partakers of the divine nature. This divine nature is godlike in nature because we are in him. When you say, "I am a partaker of this," you can say, "I am godlike."

This life is also considered to be eternal life. We can enjoy the taste of eternal life here and now even though we are not eternal now. In this life, we are able to enjoy the benefits of the eternal life. We are supposed to live life to its fullest the way God intended. We are unable to experience the fullness of the life God intended because we don't believe God said it, we think we don't deserve it, and so on. The scripture says we must believe God is and that he rewards those who seek him. I am still taking hold of the truth in my heart about this very thing. Here is the thing: either Jesus and God are liars and the biggest deceivers that ever were, or we have been given this life in us.

John said those who believe are given the right to become the sons and daughters of God. God has a wonderful plan of life for us all and sometimes we miss it. Would not it be sad if we never received it and we just perished? I want to tell everyone please do not choose the life you want and give up the life that is so much better for everybody. We think what we choose somehow does not affect anyone else. That is wrong. This is the very reason the scriptures have been written. They were written for our sakes. God really does love us.

How do we access this life we have been given? Is it something we can just take? Yes and no. Let me try to explain. Our own *hearts* deceive us throughout our lives. Sin comes from desires that we create. We have choices in this life and, sometimes, we do not make the right ones. We are told to guard the boundaries we set up in our hearts. We are told that what we meditate on is who we become. In turn, we are who we are all the way to the cells in our bodies.

Again, sometimes we make the wrong choices and reap what we have sown. It is a good thing to be corrected, if we can receive it. Then we can benefit from the correction. Correction is never bad, except when we do not like it and will not receive it. What we want to do many times is become offended at the person trying to help us. This has nothing to do with the person. What has the most potential to help us can be offensive. Offence can ruin your life, and destroy you and everyone around you. The scriptures say that a fool despises correction. It also says they who observe lying vanities forsake their own mercy. We do not always like being told what we need in life. I am telling you the truth; correction is not as bad as losing your life. Jesus said if we save our lives, we will lose them, and if we lose our lives, we will gain life.

There is a thief who is always trying to take our lives away from us. The scriptures say the thief comes to steal, kill, and destroy. The thief is offence. I know I have been the worst in the world to take offence; it has almost destroyed my life. Let me tell you all about it. I was an associate pastor at my home church. My wife for twenty years was killed in a car accident. I was grieving over this very badly. I did not realize that I was grieving, but of course I was. I thought no one really tried to help me see I was about to make the worst mistakes of my life. I went through excruciating pain and grief for the choices I made. Many people offended me by the things they had done to me and how they treated me. I was warned by the Lord in a dream what was about to happen to me. Listen, it's not just what people have done to me; it is what I have done to myself. I went through about eight years of punishment and grief. I did not think people could be so evil. All the people I trusted and believed in betrayed me from every angle.

Actually, change was about to come to my life. It could be good or bad; that was up to me. I would not take anything for the things I have learned. I will say this: I wish I hadn't let the thief steal and destroy my life. My heart became hard from the things that happened to me. They hardened me in the wrong way. What do I mean in the wrong way? Well, we can be hard of heart in the right way. The scriptures say that we should guard our hearts. Guarding means putting up boundaries in our hearts. That comes from hardening our hearts. We can harden them to help or to hurt ourselves. We have an amazing responsibility that most will never be able to see. I pray that we do see and that we can experience the life God intended for us.

We need to understand a lot of things that can help or hurt us. When we look at scriptures, we find in the Hebrew the word *nephesh* and the Greek word *zoe*. They both refer to life, from physical to spiritual. When God breathed life into Adam, the scriptures say that Adam became a living soul (nephesh). It did not say Adam became a living spirit. Most of us have been taught that the soul is immortal. This is not true. We are also taught the soul is the mind, will, and emotion. This is very sad. The soul has in it the mind, will, and emotions, but it also has wisdom, understanding, passion, desire, appetites, and emotion. Life (zoe) in the

Greek is the same. It is the same in the Greek *psuche*. Zoe, soul, and life are the same. The person is a living soul and in the person is the essence of who and what he or she is. If we can understand, we will come to realize what and who we are and how we were created. What type of beings are we? This, in turn, will help us to understand how important it is understand the life of God.

When we think about this life and how to live it, we need to understand the responsibility we have to ourselves and to everyone we have ever met or will ever meet. We could talk about teaching ourselves how to think and believe all day. Believing is the most important part; thinking and mediating is how we come to believe. What we focus on the most is what we become. Just remember: we are what we believe. These are our lives that we live on a daily basis. Some think that the hand that we have been dealt is what we get. This is not true at all, God has given us grace, his ability to work from the heart to change anything in our lives. It is up to us what kind of lives we have and what kind of lives we live. We can choose to live happy lives as we were meant to do.

Here is something important: some of us do not realize healing is a part of the life. There are a many dynamics to healing, but all of them come from God's spirit. How do we explain God's spirit? We have the scriptures and experience from living them out daily. This brings life to us. The scriptures also provide proof that the healing is real. What are some of the dynamics of healing? There are physical aspects of healing. Faith plays the biggest part in this. Faith brings things into reality. Trust is faith. God said we must believe that he is and that he rewards those who seek him. YHWH gives us a challenge. He says we should come and taste and see that he is good. We cannot learn to trust if we don't experience. What do I mean by experience? What would you say? How do you experience God on a personal level? Is that possible? It is just like being in any other relationship. Sometimes things feel great, and other times they do not. As with marriage, we do not divorce over nothing. Actually, we do not divorce at all, ever. We do not quit, and we never give up. The scriptures say that at first discipline seems grievous but afterwards it yields the peaceful fruits of righteousness.

Life is about choices; we have been given all things that pertain to life and godliness. The choice is up to us. We can choose our own ways, or we can choose the life of God. There are many costs in this walk with God, but it is worth it to gain life rather than lose it. The messiah asked what happens if we gain the whole world and lose our lives and souls.

How does fellowship with God work? Does God speak to us? I have a friend who believes we cannot talk to God at all. He believes God only speaks through the Bible. I would like to talk a little about that. God talks all the time. Actually, he never stops talking to us. This includes the lost and the unbelievers. My friend would say God speaks through us to others through the scriptures. This is not what the scriptures teach at all. The scriptures say God will reprove the world by speaking by his spirit to show their sin. He said the believer would be convicted of righteousness. He would testify of the messiah. The only reason we would not hear would be our hard hearts. When life is stolen from us, it is because of hard hearts. The life of God is stolen from us because of the boundaries we put up. This is all a hard heart is: boundaries. Boundaries stop God from reaching us and stop us from getting out. As I have already said, this limits life for us.

This chapter is about life itself. We are talking about healing on a physical level and a spiritual level. We heal from the inside out not from the outside in. That is why we must have fellowship with our father. What's the point of talking to someone if the person never talks back to us? We must believe that God talks back to us. Yes, this is true, but how? God uses many ways: our dreams, our thoughts, other people, situations, and so on. Don't forget: he said to put on trial every spirit to see if it is of

God or not. We must learn how to hear God; it is a process. It takes time to learn how to sharpen our senses. Meditation is one of the best ways to do this. If today, you hear his voice, do not harden your heart. Why is it so important to hear God for healing? He says in his word that he sent his word and healed them (Psalm 107:20). The scriptures say that the word itself is alive (Hebrews 4:12). Have we ever thought about what it means that the word is alive? His spirit is in his word and is working in us alive. It looks around in us and works to bring life to us. It can also bring death if we reject its healing process. The choice we make brings death, not the word of God. Rejecting God does not bring healing; it does the opposite. When we begin to realize the change that God brings to us, we should want more. Sometimes it means that our hearts are revealed in us. To look at them and realize who we are can be very painful. This causes grief. The longer we wait, the harder our hearts become. We use what others have done to us to delay God's healing process.

Most of the time, people don't even know what they have done to us. That is not the most important part. What is this doing to us? It brings death instead of life and healing. How do we not understand this is God speaking to us? Messiah said this is how the judgment works: the light comes and reveals the darkness, but we reject the light because our deeds are evil. I know it is a fearful thing to fall into the arms of a living God. If we want his healing, we must allow this process. Most of the time, we don't even see this working because we play religious games with God. We think our deeds are good for us. I go to church every time the doors are open. I read my Bible every day. I pray three times a day. I know we should live our lives doing these things, but they are dead works if we don't allow the process of healing. The Bible says we should move on from repenting for dead works. Repenting from dead works is the beginning of the process; we are supposed to move on and not look back. It's all about fellowship without being in a living fellowship with YHWH.

Did you know the scriptures say a merry heart does good like medicine? How we see every day means everything. How we respond to everyday life is key. I know that when we get up, we should start the day believing the day will be great. We should be thankful for everything we have and who we are in the Messiah. This is how we activate the spirit of YHWH. Doing this brings healing to our minds and bodies. The life of God from the spirit of God brings quality from the one who gives the life.[5] Can you imagine the quality of life that God has to offer? We really can't unless we experience it and live it. The scriptures say he can do more than we can ask or think according to the power that works in us.

I don't think we really understand we have the power working in us. How do we access the power we have in us? We do this through trust and experience on the journey. There are no formulas for this. Every person must find his or her own way. There are not many ways; there is only one way. It's our belief systems that make it different for each one of us. Learning to hear God is the key for all of us. It is like healing unless we know that God loves us. We learn to trust him. It is very tough to experience healing. It is very difficult to receive anything form God without knowing he loves us. Doubt and trust can't work together. We will remain unstable and our direction unsure. Of course, we will have degrees of doubt in our lives as we grow, learn, and develop.

The scripture says we should be transformed by renewing our minds. This transformation is really like a caterpillar changing into a butterfly. Metamorphose is what the scriptures are saying to us. We become something else entirely. Jesus said we cannot take the new and pour it into the old or the old will burst. We must become new creatures or new types of being. The scripture also says we change from glory to glory. This is not to say from level to level. We don't change in levels; we change in states of being. The change doesn't happen from the outside in; it is from the inside

---

[5] Thayer, 273.

out. God does not want a doer of the word; he wants a being of the word. He wants a lasting change, something that comes out of who we are not what we do. For example, if we allow change in our hearts and establish boundaries (Proverbs 23:7; Proverbs 4:23), this will bring about lasting change. It has always been about who we are and not what we do. What good is change to us if it is only by deeds? Deeds only last as long as we are doing them. Most of us think if we live good lives, that will be enough. Jesus said unless our righteousness exceeds what is on the outside, it is not acceptable. Our goal should be to allow the change to be permanent, or change is no good to us. Change, if not permanent, only brings dead works. Remember, good works benefit others, but unless those works are alive and coming from who we are, they are no good to us.

5

THE SPIRIT OF GOD AND
THE CONSCIENCE

PAUL SAYS THE SPIRIT OF GOD AND THE CONSCIENCE MUST AGREE together. He also says we can't void our consciences. The scripture says that we should never lie against the truth, no matter how we live our lives. This is where things become really good and exciting. What is the conscience? Sometimes people seem to end up without one. They are not taught to have consciences, but that does not mean they don't have them at all. We are taught by people around us: family, parents, and so on. We are taught how to see and feel about life and the things around us. This has everything to do with perception and perspective.

What is the difference between the two? Let's establish the difference. Perception is your understanding and/or interpretation of people, situations, and the world; it's your mental impression. Perspective, on the other hand, is the angle you are looking from or your point of view. How we see things governs our lives every day. The scriptures talk about Jesus perceiving people's thoughts. Was that supernatural? It could have been. He was a prophet, priest, and king. Perceiving is understanding, but it is also revelation knowledge. It is the way we understand things. What we don't understand is how important it is to see the correct way.

Did you know that Jeffery Dahmer, at the age of four, had a traumatic and painful recovery following a surgery to correct a double hernia?

This seemed to change the boy. The birth of his younger brother also affected him and he became increasingly withdrawn. His family seemed to move frequently. This also would have had an effect on him seeing and experiencing instability. His parents divorced when he was fourteen. This could have been the catalyst as it is around the time of his first murder. [6]

People are told that people are born psychopaths. There could not be anything farther from the truth. One way or the other, psychopaths develop into how and who they are. We are trained how to think and believe about everything. Remember what the scriptures say: train a child in the way he or she will go and the child will not depart from it. This is a proven fact everyone should know. If you are raising a child, it is very important. You should put your best into your child before he or she reaches the age of seven. Here is the concerning part, most would say. I only have 2,555 days to get this right. Yes, these are the most important times in training your child. In the Parable of the Sower, the seed is the most important part. What do you have growing in your heart? The development of your child will tell on itself when the word of God is given (Hebrews 4:12). The word of God reveals what is in our hearts. The choice is given to accept or reject the word of God.

Some people become very excited when they first hear the word of God, but it has not taken root in them. In other words, they have nothing in their hearts. The word will not remain with them. The word of God can bring change, but this must be at the heart level. Salvation must be accepted in the heart. The scriptures say that salvation must be in the heart. Out of the fullness of the heart, the mouth speaks. If you want a good example, think about when you are very upset and words are coming out of your mouth. You might want to listen to what you are saying. What

---

[6] Colin McEvoy, "Jeffrey Dahmer," Biography, last updated September 15, 2023, https://www.biography.com/crime/jeffrey-dahmer#childhood-and-family.

is coming out of your mouth is coming out of the abundance of your heart.

Have you ever heard people say, "Tell me how you really feel"? Feeling comes from the heart. Emotions can also come from the heart, but feeling something is much deeper. You may have also heard people say, "This is how it makes me feel." This comes from the depths of the heart. We need to listen at this point. Whether they are right or wrong, this is truly how they really see things from the heart perspective. A person's true point of view comes from the heart. The heart is never iffy; it is always a sure thing. It shows a person's pattern of acting and speaking on a consistent basis.

Have you heard people say practice makes perfect? Well, practice makes permanent. When something is in the heart, it becomes who we are. It becomes how we think, how we act, and how we live our lives.

Now we have discussed how and why we are the way we are. Where does the conscience and the spirit of God work in all this? The scriptures say that God is a spirit and those who worship him must worship in spirit and truth. What is a spirit? Some say a spirit is like the wind; you can't see it with your eyes unless you see it in a person's action. If you want to know another way to see the spirit, it is in the scriptures. The scriptures say that that the word of God is alive. It discerns thoughts and the intents of the heart. The word of God is alive, and it becomes our gauge. If you want to know how to see the spirit of God, read the word of God. The scriptures also say these words are spirit and life. The only way we can know if someone is telling us the truth about God is to gauge it by the scriptures.

Sometimes, people's use of the scriptures is twisted to appear to be true. Then we must use the whole of scripture to try the spirits to see whether they are of God. What do I mean by the whole of scripture? This means when something is the same from one end of the Bible to the other. That is the whole of scripture. These can be called Bible doctrines. You know there are people who don't believe that everything comes from the scriptures. All knowledge, wisdom, and understanding come from the scriptures. Someone might ask about this or that. I guarantee you if you have the questions, the Bible can answer them.

How do we understand God? The Bible says we can't. We can know him in many ways, but God told Job there was no way he could understand his decisions. He told him he could not know because he could not know everything that was going on. God also asked Job if he was there when he made the Pleiades in all their beauty (Job 38:31). He asked if he was there when he weighed the balances of the earth in his hands. He asked if he was there when he put the gates on the seas. There was no way for Job to understand if he was not involved in the decisions.

We have established we cannot know the reason for God's every decision. I have heard people say that God would be a schizophrenic if he brought judgment on someone and sent Jesus to take our judgment. The whole truth is God has placed judgment on Jesus. He has given us salvation as a free gift. We must decide whether we accept this gift and experience the blessings or not. Judgment has already been decreed. Whatever you sow you will also reap. God is not mocked. There will be judgment at the final day, but until then, we reap what we sow. Until then, we have the choice to live any way we choose.

We must build an understanding of the spirit of God and the conscience and understand how they both work. It doesn't matter what we want to believe. What matters is the real truth. What we believe matters according to the outcome of lives. How we see or understand matters. The reason for writing this book is to bring an understanding how the spirit of God works. We must understand the most basic Bible doctrine of the new covenant: Jesus took our judgment. God works everything he does with us in our walks. We want be able to understand that he is for us. Whether or not we can be in his presence is not based on our behavior.

I have heard people say if you have sin in your life, you want to have your prayers answered. The whole point of going into God's presence is to receive help. Being in the light causes us to make choices about how to live our lives. The word is also the light. Jesus is the word and the light. The light brings judgment or correct judgment. We choose if we are going to follow the light or continue in darkness. This darkness brings death here and forever if we don't allow change to bring life and light. These two can't be separated; light and life are synonymous. As we begin to understand these most basic things, we begin to see God in the correct way. Then we understand how he speaks to us and how he thinks about us. This causes us to hear properly or to listen.

The conscience and the spirit can say the same thing, if you have the right things in your heart. God says in his word fear is the beginning of knowledge or understanding. Being conscious of something is being aware or being awake. In Ephesians 5:14, Paul writes, "Wake up, sleeper." This means become conscious and aware. When we come to the realization by experience, we reap what we sow. God does not get us; our choices do. Not being afraid about the things of God makes us fools. We have lost our governor, our lighthouse at sea. We will crash into the rocks and be thrown into the sea. The law is our governor. It should be written in our hearts, and that will bring us to Christ.

The scriptures say that the law enslaved people and held them captive. If a person broke something, he or she had to pay. That is what leads us to Christ: he paid for us. The payment for breaking the law is death. That is why Christ died for us. The law cannot hold us in fear of death anymore, so we are free. We are free from the penalty of the law. If God hadn't wanted us to follow the law, why in this new covenant did he say, "I will put my laws in their hearts, and I will write them on their minds" (Hebrews 10:16). We are of the new covenant if we have accepted Christ as our Lord and Savior.

We talked about the seed sower earlier on. This is where the rubber meets the road. I remember when I first started on my journey, or when I decided to be serious about it. I had gone to church most of my young life and put the scriptures inside myself. The messiah said, "You search the scriptures thinking you have eternal life, and they testify me, but you will not come to me that you may have life" (John 5: 39–40). We must have the messiah abiding in us. It helps if we have the scriptures sown into us from a young age. But here's the thing: Just because we haven't spent time learning how the messiah lives in us doesn't mean there is no hope. We must persist until we bear fruit in our lives. If we don't have something built in us, we must pray that God can help us. Without something built, there is nothing to work with. A conscience you will have, but a proper one you will not.

We already talked about guarding our hearts and how important it is. Our consciences remind us to stay true to our hearts. If we have allowed God to be an influence in our lives and to write on our hearts, then we will have something to work with. The law should be written in our hearts and on our minds. This is what keeps us and what will guide and guard us from the world and its ways. It will also keep us from trouble. The law was designed around loving God and loving humankind. How could anyone say we should not follow it? The law should work from love in the heart. We should never try to force anyone to obey the law. The scriptures say that every person should work out his or her own salvation with fear and trembling.

Where and how does the spirit of God work in all this? The scriptures say that the conscience and the spirit of God should work together. Paul said he did things with a clear conscience and in the spirit of God. Messiah said that God is a spirit and those who give him value and worth should do that in spirit and in truth. When we consider what a spirit is, we find many explanations. We find that the influence of the spirit teaches us a rational way of seeing things. We must have rational minds that cause actions to work from love in our hearts. The truth comes from the scriptures. Truth is in the law, in Messiah, and in the prophets. The scriptures say that all scripture is given by inspiration of God or is God breathed. In essence, when we allow the word (spirit) to work in us, we allow God's spirit to work in us. This comes from the truth of God's word. Messiah says these words are spirit and they are truth. They are life and light for us to see with. The scriptures give us Messiah. We accept him in our hearts, and he becomes life and light to us.

We have always tried to make the spirit of God to be something weird. It is not something weird. It is very logical and reasonable to follow God from his word. We build trust as we walk out the word on our journeys. We continue and we will find true freedom through our experiences. The more we walk, the more we see (understand) and know there is really no other way. God's instruction to "come taste and see that I am good" becomes reality. The more we experience the things God says, the more real they become. We will be doing his will on earth as it is in heaven. His kingdom will be made manifest in the earth for others to follow. The kingdom works from the inside of us and is manifested by the fruit we produce. That fruit shows people God is real, and he rewards those who seek him.

The price we pay is worth it when we see the benefit it brings: peace. Peace works toward the common good of all humankind. God wants us to know how his spirit works in humankind. That way, there is no confusion because God is not the author of confusion. His plan is for us to be unconfused about how to have true lives. He says, "I know the plans I have for you, to prosper you" (Jeremiah 29:11). He wants us to prosper in health and life. In other words, he wants us to have happy, fulfilled lives. Messiah said he came to give us life in its fullness.

Things will be difficult as we live our lives because of the way a fallen world works around us. We can still have peace in our walks if we listen. Listening is a lot different than hearing. Listening means hearing and acting from our hearts in love. Don't take it lightly when you say someone is for us and not against us. He has never been against us in any form or fashion. He loves us so much he has never given up on us or left us. He never changes; he is always the same. The cycle runs in circles not straight lines. Have you ever heard "what goes around comes around"? Everything comes back around; as we sow things, so we will reap. We can enjoy reaping or we can suffer reaping, depending on what we sow. It always has and it always will come back to us. Whatever we give, we get, whether we like it or not.

As for me, I want to like it and enjoy my life. I pray I will always listen and give it my all to plant good seeds in my life and others' lives. Don't forget: do not listen to the lies people will say to try to draw you away from God and his word, which is where all good things come from. Let's give God his due and enjoy life to its fullest. I promise we will never be ashamed when we stand before our God and father. We then will hear him say, "Well done my good and faithful servant. Go into life eternal" (Matthew 25:23). God has such mighty plans for us. We can't even imagine how good they will be because we live in a fallen world with fallen people. It is so hard to see what it would be like to live where all people are doing the will of the father.

6

CONSCIOUS AWARENESS

WHAT IS CONSCIOUS AWARENESS? I THINK WE ALL REMEMBER THE trees and the Garden of Eden, where Adam and Eve made a choice that would affect us all. The tree of the knowledge of good and evil led them to become consciously aware of evil and good. They decided for themselves what was good and what was evil. They decided for themselves to make choices without God involved. I think we all know what a placebo is. Well, let's not get ahead of ourselves. Let us really investigate what happened in the garden.

First, let's envision the garden. What does scripture mean when it says "garden"? It is a location. A fence surrounded it, so there was no going outside. It was fenced in or had boundaries in place. This was not to hold them prisoners. There was a whole planet to dwell on, however, they were protected from not becoming aware of until they were ready to take care of the whole planet. The garden was a training ground with choices. The tree of life would be where Adam and Eve trusted God. In turn, they would live forever with all things provided for them. They would have no worries. The garden had everything they would ever need to eat and they could enjoy it with pleasure.

Then there is the tree of knowledge of good and evil. This tree would set them free to decide for themselves what is right and wrong in living life without God's help. It has always been about trust with God. God

41

will and can provide everything we will ever need or want if we trust him to do so.

Adam was content to do this, but Eve was not. Eve began to talk with Satan and listen to his counsel. He told her that if they ate from the tree of knowledge, they could determine what was right and wrong for themselves. They would be like gods. Eve decided for herself to put this to the test. She decided to see what it was like to have independence and live life the way she decided. Adam was drawn into it because of his love for his wife. I don't understand how Eve could lead her husband into this because she knew the truth immediately after she ate the fruit. She gave it to her husband knowing. This is becoming consciously aware. She became aware the moment after she ate. Do I blame Eve? Yes and no. We can't rule out the fact that Adam had a choice. I know they were both aware after the fact because they were ashamed and hid themselves.

Becoming aware is something we need to consider. Some things are better left unknown. If Adam and Eve had known what it would cause for them, and what it did to us, they would have left that tree alone. Repeatedly, we move into this way of thinking where we forget that there are costs in the choices we make.

We have a responsibility to think before we act. All our choices affect those around us.

We become conscious or awake, as Messiah would say. We have heard prophets say those who sleep should wake. I remember when I awoke from my sleep. It began when I started reading the scriptures. I started in the beginning of the scriptures. I read the old in the morning and the new in the evening. I began to wonder how I didn't see all those things until then. I had not become consciously aware of the reality of God. I had not had a real fellowship with him. Messiah said if we continue in his word, we shall know the truth (experience the truth) and the truth will make us free. The word *free* here means unrestrained, not bound by obligation. As we become aware consciously of the price that Messiah paid, we become free of the law's condemnation. We are free to experience the Lord God in a personal way that we could not before. The scriptures say that God is reconciling us to himself through this love. It is very hard for us to believe that a holy God can love sinners like us. Until we become aware that it is not how good or how bad we are, we cannot have or experience God in a real conscious state. We can say we know God all day long without becoming consciously aware on a spiritual level. Experiencing something on a spiritual level means that our rational minds think of things in practical ways. This makes the experience normal, like getting up out of bed in the morning, walking across the floor, or eating food. This is when the spiritual person knows the spirit of God in a natural way. It is no longer far off for us to have an experience that changes our lives.

The only way to know God is to have an awakening experience with him. This is how we become consciously aware or awaken from sleep. We continue to be awakened as we walk in what he has told us. God says, "Come taste and see that I am good." I have spent most of my life putting the things of God to the test the way he asked us to. We are always making life so hard that we can't reach them. I know of some ways this happens.

We can start with how people jump around or say, "Hey, I like this feeling." How does this affect our everyday lives on a practical level? If something doesn't help us to apply the words of God in a practical way, what good is it? Emotions are never important unless they enable us to apply God's ways to our lives in practical ways. In other words, applying God's word should become normal in our everyday lives.

Not caring at all also hinders us. We can have traditions or patterns of worship. An emotional connection with God is also important. The word of God is alive unless we make it subject to tradition. Messiah said we should not behave as hypocrites do and use memorized prayers. That behavior doesn't have an emotional connection to a living God.

Some religions have only a formula for worship that does not involve experiencing God. Messiah said when on the last day, these people came to him, he would tell them to depart because he never knew them.

There is another way we can say I am the righteousness of God. It doesn't matter what I do. I am right with God because of Messiah. This is true, but without knowing him, it is unacceptable to God. As we have just seen, we must know him and he us. If we don't know someone, how do we trust him or her? We sometimes believe it is good enough to know about God, but this is never going to be true. Paul said he could know all things, but without love, he would only be like a beating drum. If we do not place value on God, we will not understand how to love him. The word *worship* could be better translated *worthship*. If we do not value him in our lives, we really have nothing.

How accurate is the saying "once I am saved, I am always saved"? There is no way this can work. First, where is the drive or the value in worship? The scriptures say that fear is the beginning of knowledge, or the beginning of knowing him on a personal level. If there is no fear of losing something, where does the value for it go? I can tell you it doesn't grow into anything. People say there is no fear in love. Well, I loved my parents, but I also knew not to do the things they told me not to do. It is the same with God. The Bible says that God is not mocked, and whatever a person sows he or she will reap.

As we become consciously aware of anything on this journey, we become more intimately fulfilled. In fact, nothing or no one can fulfill us; only God can. Without understanding or knowing this, we will be most miserable. We will also make others miserable trying to obtain the fulfillment we desire. Have you ever heard someone say, "My job is not my source"? Nothing should be your source. Only God can fulfill you to the fullest.

When we become consciously aware, the only way we can be fulfilled is through our Father and God. This settles it for me. You talk about not putting so much pressure on your husband, wife, or children. Not even your friends can fulfill you. Let us say you're a single man. Every time you see a woman with the right features, you think you would like to have her. You have her, then you find out she doesn't have anything you wanted. You start looking for another woman, but you will never find her. She does not exist. What you're looking for comes from God and him only. What do I mean? How can God fulfill me better than a beautiful woman? Answer this question. Are you a happy person without God in your life? No, you are not, and you will always be looking for something or someone else to make you happy.

It has always been funny how, when I buy a truck, it seems to be what I want in every way. Then I see something that someone else has on his or her truck, and suddenly I want a new truck.

How does God fulfill us? Paul says he had much and had little, but he learned to be content in whatever state he was in. I traveled a lot a few years back. Wherever I went seemed like home. Someone asked why I felt that way. At first, I didn't really know what made me feel at home. I found out later it was because I was content wherever I went and whatever I did.

I bought a dog, a redbone. When I first got him, he was so little. I asked if I could have the runt in the litter of puppies. I had been told the runt was always the best dog. That is what I wanted the runt. I brought him home and when I would feed him, he would go crazy for the food. It was like he had never eaten. I would refill his bowl and he would eat it all. No matter how many times I refilled his bowl, he would eat the food very fast. I told a friend of mine what he was doing. My friend said he had a poor man's mentality. I said, "What? A poor man's mentality?" I was taken aback that he would talk like that about a dog.

I was about to learn something. I asked him what to do. He said to fill a five-gallon bucket with dog food. I should make sure I had enough water as well. I had two big five-gallon buckets full of water and food. I thought the dog would blow up. That is what I thought every time I filled his bowl. He ate so much that he became sick. My friend was right; he had a poor dog mentality. It wasn't long until I took away the bucket and gave him a regular dog bowl.

You see, the dog had been taught to believe he would not be able to eat. All the bigger dogs would keep him from having his mother's milk. When they were weaned, the bigger dogs kept him out. He learned if he didn't push in and get food, he would starve. I went through the same experience having a poor man's mentality. I watched my grandfather go outside and chop wood in the dead of winter. It was cold, and his hand would chap and burst open. I thought, *Man, what a good grandpa who would go out and do that to keep us warm.*

Let me tell you what I learned. I did not want to do that when I got old. However, I had no idea how not to think the exact way as my grandfather. I had become consciously aware of my grandpa and his suffering. He was so good and kind. He was very quiet most of the time. I loved him very much. He could pray as if he was in the throne room. You knew this because of the way he talked to God. He had a personal relationship with the father. I always prayed that I could learn to pray like he did.

I became consciously aware of wanting to pray the way my grandfather had done. He was also very knowledgeable about the scriptures. I learned a lot from him. I have always checked people out. He was very close to the truth of God's word. Some people never get it; they always go after the wrong understanding because that comes from lust of their own hearts.

Ego and conscious awareness raise a big question. The ego is the part of the mind that mediates between the conscious and the unconscious. It is responsible for a sense of personal identity. Ego defines your sense of self; it allows you to be aware of yourself as a person separate from everyone else. Ego is your personality and your identity. It is what you think of yourself.

Your ego is running on programs from your subconscious mind. Most of these programs are created in your childhood. Limiting thoughts are the result of these ego programs. Every time you believe these limiting thoughts, you reinforce these programs.

What we think about all day long is up to us. We have the power to control these thoughts. It is the power of choice. The power of choice will help us or hurt us. It is better to err on the side of mercy. Ego is the me factor or the self. Ego focuses on what the individual wants, what the individual feels, how others make him or her feel, and what others are doing to him or her. Can we kill the ego? That is the question we should all be asking. Can I deal with dying to myself? Is the right thing to die to myself? How would I do that? Is it really possible?

You become what you think about all day long. As you think in your heart, so you are. We can stop thinking what we think all day. We can also start thinking about something different, something better. Is it important to become aware of yourself and who you are? I think it can be really a good thing. When we are being disciplined by our parents, we think they do not like us. We felt like they did not want us to have any fun.

As I have become older, I have begun to realize that no matter how they went about it, they were right to protect me and guide me. If you really want to see the truth, you need to seek it out. Messiah said unless someone loses his or her life, he or she will not save it. I could write a book about the ego and self-awareness. We want to save humankind, not get rid of it. Should we only think of ourselves and not consider others? Could we give our lives for someone else? I think that would be hard to do with self in the way.

47

Just what is it we are looking for? I know my neighborhood in the city has grown so very much over the past few years. I like a lot of things about the growth. It gives a lot of people a chance to enjoy our community. Here is the thing: there is hardly any room in our city for people to be. So many new people have moved here, the ones of us who live here now cannot really enjoy the city. People will not govern themselves unless governed by others if ego is first. In other words, people would not stop wanting and getting unless someone says, "Stop." Everybody just wants what he or she wants. The problem is no one thinks he or she is hurting anything or anyone.

Have you ever heard "you shall not covet" or "I am content with whatever state I am in"? I really enjoy my life and the things I have. People everywhere are doing what James said: they war and fight among themselves. Do they not come from your own desire (James 4:1)? He says all we must do is ask. People ask and have not because they ask with the wrong motives. Our motives are everything. What is motivating you to do what you do? Is your motive coming from love or does it come from selfish greed?

When we wake up about something, sometimes it is like a light just turned on. Sometimes it is like, *Oh man, I can't believe I was treating people that way to get what I want.* We should always think about things we are doing, and we should consider our motives. God has a great plan for us if we follow it.

7

WHAT IS THE ANOINTING?

WHAT IS THE ANOINTING? IS IT SOMETHING ON THE INSIDE OF US? IS it something that is on us? Why is the anointing important? I hope to answer these and many other questions. I pray God gives me the wisdom and understanding to do so. I have seen many people want the anointing of God on their lives. I have seen many people misrepresent the anointing. The anointing has always been given to priests chosen to represent God on the earth. They become God's mouthpieces. When Arron was chosen as the leading high priest, Moses poured olive oil over his head until it ran down and dripped from his beard.

When David was anointed king of Israel, Samuel, the priest, prophet, and judge poured the oil over him. Samuel was called by God when he was a little boy. One night while he was in bed, God called to him. Samuel was given by his mother to the priest Eli. Hannah, his mother, asked God for a son. She told God if he would give her a son, she would give him to the priest to raise.

Understanding the anointing is not very difficult. We make it difficult. God has his own business, and the anointing is his business. Sometimes we want to think we have a right to make it our business. I have seen so many things take place when it comes to these types of things. God chooses whomever he pleases to give out his word. God's anointed have always been the ones who stand up for the truth. They are always the

49

shepherds of God's people, the protectors of the ways of the Father. What did Messiah say? "I say what my father says."

I would never lay the name God's anointed on myself unless, like Messiah, I was told to do so. The spirit of the lord is *on* me because the Lord has anointed me. What does it mean to be anointed? How does that work? It means to smear or rub with oil, to consecrate to an office. It means being set apart to do the work of the Lord. In other words, Messiah was saying his Father set him apart to do what he had been planning for years.

A lot of people want to make this a much bigger deal of this than what it is. Some people think they can elevate themselves to an office. There is a preacher I know very well. I know he has put himself on a pedestal and given himself status. He calls himself a prophet of God who speaks for God. Do I really have the right to call this person out? Yes, we are all called to challenge. The scriptures say to preach the word instantly in season and out of season. We should reprove, rebuke, and exhort with all long suffering. This gives me the right to do so, and do it when it feels good and when it doesn't.

God has a way he likes to do things and we really can't change the way that works. Sometimes, we just want to set ourselves up on high, to make ourselves gods and lords over God's people. Peter warned us not to do this because we have no right. I had a pastor who wanted to do that. He said to me one day, "You're going to have to decide who you're going to follow: me or God." Of course, you know what I said: "I am going to follow God." He then set out to destroy my life. This prophet I was telling you about earlier did the same thing. He and his clan didn't like it when I called them out using the scriptures.

The anointing we have is amazing; it carries with it everything. An anointing is on us and in us. Both serve a purpose to equip the believer. God is all about equipping his children to live life and be full of joy.

There are two types of anointing: anointing on us and in us; both do different things. The anointing on someone is for the equipping of the ministry. The anointing in us also equips us for life. I have talked to you about that some in past chapters. I want to talk a little more here. We want to realize that anointing in us brings life and power. It is connected to grace; we can't have one without the other. Some would say that grace is only unmerited favor. It isn't, so we need to look at the word *grace*. The word *grace* means the power of God that works from the heart to makes us able to live our lives as God intended.

This is the anointing from the inside; it works from the heart. God doesn't care about our actions when it comes to living right. He is only ultimately after real and lasting change. God wants us to have the best in our lives; that has always been his plan. What do we really want? This is the real question. We need to answer this question. It is very simple. Do you want to live for God or do you want to live for yourself? We should care enough about ourselves to want God's ways. He is our creator. He created us and gave us this life to live to its fullest. Nothing is holding us back, but it has always been our choice we should realize that. We have the power to walk with our heads held high as the children of the living God, without shame or devices holding us down. Those devices are powerless in him.

I had this dream one time. I was in my back yard. I walked off the back porch. The devil was standing in front of me and he looked scary. I thought to myself, *What does he want?* My little dog was behind him, barking up a storm. The devil wasn't moving at all, so I walked around behind him. I saw what my dog was trying show me. You have seen those life-like stands of people in stores. I have been standing by one and said, "Excuse me" before I realized what it was. This is what I saw as I walked around the devil. I realized I did not have to be afraid of the devil. He had no backing. We are the problem, not our friends, the devil, or our families. God is not our problem; he is on our side and not against us. We have an anointing inside of us that comes from God and gives us power to overcome.

This anointing teaches us all things because it abides with in us. It continues to teach and work to give us lives full of the riches of his goodness. Ego loves hindering this. Ego only promotes our own fame and the "what about me" syndrome. Look out when someone tries to promote you saying flattering things to you. The person wants to put you on a pedestal so later he or she can knock you off. Just say thanks and move on.

Where was I? I was trying to say how the anointing works inside us to bring the life God intended. We have been given all things that pertain to life and godliness. Let us use all the tools we have to our advantage.

The other type of anointing is the one that is placed on us for the work of the ministry. God says in his word many are called but few are chosen. We undergo a training process to be ready for being chosen. This is for ministry, not being saved; salvation is a gift from God. Ministry is something we are chosen to do that God sets us apart to do. Being set apart is totally different. Being set apart means you are ready for the master's use. Paul spent two years in the desert learning before he actually started ministering. Jesus spent a lifetime so he could preach the gospel for three years of his life.

Many times, we miss the point and miss our opportunities to preach what God has given us to say to the people. The anointing can leave and return to a person's life. I was at a funeral one day. I saw the anointing, or the spirit of God, come in and rest on this man as he ministered to the people. As soon as the man reached the point when comfort was achieved, the anointing, or the spirit of God, left. Many things come with the spirit of God or the anointing to equip us to minister.

God wants his people comforted and helped. We don't always know how to do that, so the spirit is our helper. God promises he will help us do this. Ministering is not something that only comes from us; it comes from our helper God's spirit. I know that a person cannot give away what he or she does not have. Without a life yielded to the Lord God, we are like dry morsels, empty of life-giving power. A man once told me that he would rather see a sermon than hear one. The anointing within us also works to help us minister. Jesus said if we continue in his word, we will know the truth and the truth will set us free. I have told you many times that the word *know* here is the word for experiential knowledge. Something that we walk through gives us a testimony to others. Without the experience, there is no power.

The word says that people would have forms of godliness but deny their power. We must realize we must go through the storm to have the power. Without the power, we cannot effectively help others. I have seen ministers who were dry. I wondered when they would stop talking. One minister continued to say in every preaching you have to love, you have to obey, and you have to serve. We don't have to do anything at all; we can do whatever we want. We have free will and God gave it to us. We have to choose to enjoy lives filled with power. We can also choose to live lives full of trouble that we create, then blame everyone else for what is wrong with us and why we can't do this or that. People can cause us problems, but it is our choice how we finish what we start.

The anointing on us and in us comes with gifts. The scriptures say that God works with people, showing signs and miracles that confirm they and God are working toward the same goal. We never self-promote. Promotion comes from the Lord on our journeys. We are empowered by and through obedience. This must work through the heart for the power to manifest the results. We either have fruit or we do not. The scriptures say that we will be wellsprings flowing over on everyone else as we grow and go.

If we really want to know how the spirit of God works, we must realize these things. This is to our benefit. Therefore, we must yield to the father in our hearts to feel and see the power manifest. Jesus said not to build a house unless we first consider the cost involved. If we do not, passersby would laugh and say we never finished what we started.

We don't want to find ourselves in this predicament.

I think there is something else we have to consider before we go on. Jesus said it is better that we have millstones tied about our necks and be thrown into the depths of the sea than to offend one of these little ones. However, he warns us three times not to be offended. Offence brings death and not life to us. It will kill us in many ways. It takes our joy, which is our strength to walk through this journey. This will cause us many troubles and make it impossible to finish the race that is set before us.

People most of the time don't even know they have offended us. Therefore, we must remember not to be offended. Offence takes our power away and makes us powerless in our walks. We can't make people pay for what they have done. Only God knows how to correct those who hurt us and help them at the same time. We should never rejoice in another's suffering. That can only come from evil hearts of unbelief.

Evil hearts of unbelief stop us and cause us to wander in dry places with no life in it. I don't like how this feels. I have lain awake at night angry, not knowing I was angry or offended. You will have no rest or peace and no way to enter into it. You will have no way to see the path clearly. Your foolish heart will be darkened. Your heart will harden. You cannot hear the Lord because you will not let him into you to heal you from a broken heart.

Jesus said he was anointed to heal the broken hearted and to set at liberty those who were oppressed. If we don't allow him, he can do nothing. Jesus said when he walked in his hometown, he could not do any mighty works because of the people's unbelief. If we do not trust our Lord and savior, he can't help us change and grow into mature people. The scriptures say Jesus gave gifts to people in order to equip the saints and bring them to maturity so they would not be tossed about by every wind of doctrine. Instead of running after all kinds of different doctrines, let us yield our hearts to God. Doctrines are good when they aid in bringing us to fellowship with the father. However, when they only add to our knowledge about God, we will never be changed from the heart. We will never experience the power to set us free from the bondage of sin. Jesus has paid a big price for to be able to have life here and after the resurrection. It would be a sad thing to gain the whole world and lose our lives in the end. I am talking about eternal life.

I want us to stop and think. Put the book down and meditate on the things of God. See what we are missing because of offence. It would really be something to stand before a living God and know we have just missed out on wonderful lives here and miss living forever with no sin, no hurt, and no mean people to deal with. There would be no more dying, no more sickness, and no more pain of people taking advantage of us for their own gain. God says in the scriptures that he will wipe away all tears from our eyes and there will be no more suffering. There will be no more badness anywhere on this planet, just happy, loving people helping one another live prosperous lives forever. What a life that would be to live. Sometimes, I feel vexed by the things going on around me, just as Lot was in Sodom because of the things going on around him. This world is indeed evil and all about self-love.

People have no respect for authority and no respect for parents. People have no mercy at all, it seems. Let us not look. Let it not stop us from receiving all that God has for us. Let's keep our eyes on the prize and don't look back. Jesus said the one who keeps looking back is not fit for the kingdom of God. Let us run the race and fight the good fight of faith as Paul told us to do. He is an example for us to follow. He said people should be his followers even as he was a follower of the Messiah.

We are encompassed with such a great cloud of witnesses. Let us lay aside the weight that easily besets us. Let's get on our feet, knock down that wall in front of us, and accomplish the goal of life. This gives us a purpose-filled life, which, in turn, gives us drive. This is what we really desire to do. It feels so good to be free of guilt and shame. This causes us to be able to look into the eyes of our friends and our enemies with love and confidence.

Do you have ears to hear and eyes to see? If we are blind and deaf, how will we finish the race when we can't find the way? We should just give in. It is worth it and has a big payment of joy, happiness, and life filled with hope, peace, and rest. We desire these things to fill our hearts. We can give them away when others see what they have done for us. Don't give up or stop no matter where you are on this journey. God's plans are greater than we can imagine. Amen!

8

HOW PEOPLE SEE THE SPIRIT OF GOD

WOW! WHAT A CHAPTER WE ARE ABOUT TO EMBARK ON. GET READY. As we get closer to the end of this book the more, we can see the climax. Answers are coming. Don't stop now, because there is just a little bit left. I am getting excited writing this book at this point. I think it is strange how people see or want to see the spirit of God. You think people would be afraid to do some of the things they do. There are videos of people making animal noises in huge churches with big name preachers. They claimed these were moves of God. There is no way to say these things because the scriptures do not condone these behaviors. I have seen people in different churches get up out of their seats and run around the auditorium. They say there is a move of God. Is it really a move of God or is it just an emotional expression of how they feel? I think we could safely say it is only their feelings being expressed. The scriptures do say we are supposed to enthusiastically praise and worship our God. I want to say that I've been to a lot of churches and I've seen a lot of things. I'm not trying to be critical or judgmental. I want to base everything I say off the truth of the scriptures. One of these people started out as a young man, I guess about nineteen years old.

I was dedicated to serving God in every way. I was dissatisfied with the church I went to at the time, so I went out to find the truth. I went to a little church on a hill in a small town. I had an experience with God. I definitely believe even today that I had an experience. As I have moved through my life, I have seen a lot of different things.

I saw people uttering what sounded like some kind of weird language. I didn't understand it. I don't know what I thought I would find at all these different churches. I think I wanted the camaraderie of the people and friendships and relationships. As I continued on my walk, I found a lot of things. I changed my view about the spirit of God, how he works, and how he governs many times. It's not really that easy figuring all these things out. It is very hard most of the time to work through these issues that you don't understand don't feel are in the scriptures.

I've spent many years trying to work my way through these things. In writing this book, I want you to see a different picture than I've ever had. It took me a lot of years to find what I'm doing in this book.

It's not been an easy task—not in the least. I wish I could make things a lot clearer. It's not easy seeing how people see some of the things and do some of the things they do. It would make things a whole lot easier if people would leave well enough alone and live by the scriptures. However, I don't think they really want to. I believe they want to make these things up for themselves. I believe it makes them feel better from a worldly standpoint. What do I mean by worldly standpoint? I mean holding on to the things they want to do. It's in whatever you want and how you want to live your life. You have to want something in order for it to work. Sometimes, we don't want things; we want them to stay the same. However, God has a different plan.

I know this: I don't want to spend my life not looking for the truth. I hope we can see how important it is to look for truth. I hope I understand it the way God wants me to. I learn every day; I hope I never stop learning.

Okay, let's get back to how people see the spirit of God. They see the spirit of God like this. They see him responsible for everything that happens. Well, I believe that things worked out just the way God planned them. Does that mean God made people do everything they have done? With this type of logical thinking, you would have to say people do not have free will. What does that mean? This means that whatever I have done, I could blame God for it or the devil or someone else and get away with it. The problem is we won't get away with it and God said we wouldn't. As a person sows, so he or she will reap. I think we really don't know how God actually thinks, so we try to figure it out. What makes God almighty God? We want to know who he is and how he works. In turn, we try to figure him out from our reasoning or something we have been taught. This doesn't work if we use our reasoning without the understanding of God's word. For example, we have been taught that the God of the Old Testament is not as good as the God of the New Testament. When we reason from that standpoint, we really can't get a proper understanding. If we really want to understand what makes God Almighty, we need to understand that when he does something or says something, he does not break his word. He is consistent in all things that he does.

The word teaches that the word will not go out and come back void. That doesn't mean it will achieve a bad result or a good result. It does, however, mean that it will cause a difference. Sometimes, hearing the word of God will harden people's hearts and sometimes it will soften their hearts. I believe that God knows our hearts and can use that to his advantage. In other words, because he knows our hearts, he knows whether he can trust us or use us. Whenever God makes a covenant with humankind, he does not interfere in breaking that covenant. God has never broken a covenant he has made, although he has fulfilled a covenant. The covenant of the law has been fulfilled in the Messiah. This is the reason the law can't condemn us now. We will never be free from the law; we still reap what we sow. I hope we realize this is what happened to

Timothy J. Brown

Adam and Eve. They reaped what they sowed. When God told them the consequences, they ate the wrong fruit and reaped.

People also see the spirit of God this way. They will say the spirit of God led me that way or this way. The spirit of God will never lead us in a way that contradicts what the scriptures say. Peter said that Paul's writings are sometimes hard to understand. Those who are unlearned and unskilled in the scriptures twist them to their own destruction.

The scriptures teach us the rules of service when we come together to worship in church. It's all about order in the service so people can know who God is. There are church services where people get up and run around the church during service. There are people speaking in tongues or other languages. I don't believe there are any reasons we should be speaking in any other language. Say, for instance, that we are in an English-speaking church. Should we have a minister speaking in Spanish? Does that make a lot of since? Most English-speaking people would not understand the minister. That is what the gift of tongues is: a gift of other languages is a gift, not something we have learned. Do you know how many people teach otherwise? They teach that it is a heavenly language, a tongue unknown to humans. This is not what the scriptures teach. The scriptures teach us that if we do not know a language, we need an interpreter. Remember what Acts, chapter 2 says? The Jews asked how they could hear Galileans in their own language. The issue is people are not taught about this properly.

People just take someone's word and never investigate the truth. Did you know that in 2009, it was concluded that there are 6,909 distinct languages on this planet?[7] Religious organizations have taken this and

---

[7] Stephen R. Anderson, "How many languages are there in the world?" Linguistic Society of America, accessed January 5, 2024, https://www.linguisticsociety.org/content/how-many-languages-are-there-world.

60

turned it into something weird, something that God did not intend and is not involved in.

The only reason people would do things like this is self-promotion. They could be ignorant of the truth. That would be a good reason, but I would never want to be ignorant. I know I have had some misunderstandings along the way in life. I also know that I will have more as I grow and learn. Everyone else will as well. I challenge you to always test the spirits to see whether they are of God.

This is the reason why we have order in the scriptures. People will do all kinds of things if there is no order. Think about Simon the sorcerer. He had been around for a while, hanging around with the apostles. Then one day, he saw a miracle being performed and he offered to buy the power the person possessed. He wanted to use it to make money and be famous. Sometimes, there are no limits to how we allow ourselves to be. Man, have we taken down the barriers. The scriptures say to guard our hearts above all else. Your heart is who you are within all your belief systems. We can even call them programs that have been built for us. We are either given good programs or bad ones. This is no metaphor; we are really trained how and what we are to believe. The program might come from an outside source, something that influences you. We have to remember to guard our hearts.

If we don't understand the spirit of God, witchcraft, sorcery, and divination can operate in familiar spirits and false prophets. Knowing his order of things will keep us from getting into trouble. You can be possessed of a spirit in order to soothsay. This is like the woman possessed by a spirit that Paul cast out. You can use the stars to predict the future and you can operate in familiar spirits.

We think many times this will never happen to me. It can and will in some cases before we realize it is happening. It happens very slowly because the heart is convinced over a period of time. In time, your heart is convinced it is okay because you have built a belief system. Again, guard your heart.

This happens along the way as you dabble a little here and a little there. The next thing you know, the matrix has you.

God reveals to us that the stars have an order. The stars tell us of the order of salvation. He discussed this with Job when he came down to tell him why he could do the things or allow the things that happened to him. He also warns us not to go to the star watchers to tell us our future. The magi came to Herod, asking if they could seek the king who had been predicted: the savior of all the world. They had been watching the stars for his arrival. They brought him frankincense and myrrh.

We can see how the stars can be used to see the future. The question is whether the magi were wrong for what they had done. I think Daniel could have been the magi's teacher and taught them about the coming of the messiah. That is only a guess; it is only a theory of mine and of some of my friends. We must be careful what we believe. I have never studied the stars, even out of curiosity. I investigated how the stars told of the coming of the Messiah because God told Job about it. I have never dabbled any further because there was no other information given to us.

I wanted to understand what God was talking about. Using the scriptures and the revelation from our God is not wrong. One of my friends went too far, picked up the study of the stars, and was making predictions. He made a few and I stopped following what he was saying. I also warned him of the danger he was messing with. He said he wanted to teach people the truth. However, God said we should not predict with and through the stars. They are called observers of times and their behavior is condemned by the Lord.

We want to believe all kinds of things are acceptable, or we just want things our way. I don't think I have ever seen someone breaking the commands of God who didn't have a selfish motive. We should always check our intents. Why am I really doing this? Am I doing this for selfish reasons? How will this benefit the Kingdom of God? Is this something God would do if he was on earth living an everyday life?

The gifts of the spirit are a very important part of the church. Some people say the gifts are no longer being given out by the Lord. That is very far from the truth. The gifts are relevant in today's world and God has not stopped giving them. We should understand the gifts of the spirit and not be ignorant about them. Paul said he did not want us to be ignorant about them. The spirit is given so all can see and profit from it.

The gifts of the spirit are wisdom, the word of knowledge, faith, the working of miracles, prophecy, the discerning of spirits, different languages, and interpretations of those languages. We are supposed to use them to aid and edify the body working together for the same purpose. They are for promoting the kingdom. Paul explains there must be order in the way they are used.

There are prophets, teachers, and miracles, gifts of healing and help, governments, and, last of all, languages. These are all given to promote the kingdom. If we are not helping the church/the people, we are doing it for the wrong reason. We must be serving the people, helping them to become disciples and grow into mature people. These gifts are given to show signs following what we are doing. It shows God is behind what we are doing. This is God's endorsement, if you will. The scriptures say these gifts show if God is backing us.

It doesn't matter how many gifts we have; if they do not operate through love, they don't do anyone any good. Paul says that love is not puffed up and does not behave in a selfish way. It doesn't seek its own way. It is not easily provoked. It doesn't think evil thoughts. It does not rejoice in lawlessness. It rejoices in the truth and handles the pressures. It believes, hopes, and endures all things for the sake of others.

We can check ourselves to see if we are following the Lord in how we live our life using gifts. God wants us to give our lives for each other and follow him in all our ways. We can end up going the wrong way and operating in familiar spirits if we are trying to promote ourselves. These giftings are put here to help us and others. What are familiar spirits? Familiar spirits are demons people work with to obtain information. People use them to play the prophet's role and say their information comes from God.

Some people believe and use these people for information. I remember a minister who operated in this way. He was getting information from demons and saying it was from God. He misled many people. I tried to help those people but they did not want my help. There was nothing I could do but pray for them. I went to this church. The church had opened itself to all preachers. I preached, then he preached, and all he was doing was trying to discredit me.

I was teaching about the heart, and he was trying to say it wasn't the heart we have problems with. He said the battle is in the mind. I knew he was uneducated and didn't understand, but he was misleading those people. The thing is they sided with him.

It is very true there is a battle in the mind, but I taught that God is after the heart. He was also prophesying over people. People were coming from everywhere to have him prophesy over them. God doesn't work like that. God lives inside the believer and the scriptures say that, because of this, we don't need anyone to teach us. God says that these things are abominations to him.

People sometimes become lost in things because they don't really want to change. They just want the power, like Simon the sorcerer. Sometimes, people seem to want to operate in spiritualism. Something supernatural is what people want rather than accept that God has plans for our lives. We must change to get it to work. First, we must be born again then receive the spirit of God into us. The spirit teaches us all things. Sometimes, we just don't like the way God asks us to go.

God is a good God, even though we don't understand it. He has great plans for us. It is not that God has a strange way of getting us from point A to point B. Our hearts are crooked or twisted, so he has to work with them to get us where we are going. We need to learn to trust him even though it doesn't feel good.

9

HOW THE SPIRIT OF GOD WORKS

GOD DOESN'T WORK IN WEIRD WAYS, AS WE THINK. GOD IS REALLY very simple in his ways, and he never changes. We need to keep this in mind throughout this chapter. He never changes; this is part of God protecting us. What does it mean that he never changes? "I think of things like "I am YHWH and I change not" (Malachi 3:6). He is faithful even when we are not. Paul wrote that God is "the same yesterday, today, and forever" (Hebrews 13:8). We think that God changes with the wind. We think he judges us every time we sin. He doesn't because of the blood of Jesus. We do reap what we sow. However, we think God is punishing us for what we have done. This is not so. God said don't be deceived. Paul also wrote that "God is not mocked. Whatsoever a man sows that will he reap" (Galatians 6:7). God isn't bringing judgment on us. It is the result of what we have done.

I used to wonder how God will ever judge the world if the blood of Jesus is shed for our sins. How will that stop? The scriptures say that it will be as it was in the days of Noah. What was it like in the days of Noah? God said, "My spirit will not always strive with man because he is also flesh" (Genesis 6:3). The scriptures say the thoughts of people's hearts were evil continually (Genesis 6:5). When the thoughts of people's hearts become evil continually, the Lord will separate the sheep from the goats.

The Spirit of the Lord is our help. I can say boldly God is my helper and I will not fear. He says, "I will strengthen you. I will help you; I will uphold you" (Isaiah 41:10). He keeps us, he is slow to anger, and he never sleeps. God "is our refuge, a very present help in trouble" (Psalm 46). He is our deliverer. He is on our side. How is God our helper? How does that work?

His Spirit lives on the inside of us. He reminds us of the truth. He first teaches us the truth, and then he reminds us. When we allow this to happen, everything works together for good according to his purpose. As our trust in him grows, the more his will manifests itself in our lives. Because the Lord is faithful, he will establish us on this journey, and he guards us from the evil one. Zechariah 4:6 states, "'It is not by might or by power but by my spirit' says the Lord." You might say you thought the Spirit of God gives us power, and it does. Things happen not by our power or strength. The joy of the Lord is my strength. We also receive his might by yielding to his Spirit. He has plans for us. They are good and not evil. He gives us a future and hope (Jeremiah 29:11). God is a spirit and those who worship him must worship him in spirit and in truth.

The scriptures say for us to seek him continually. This simply means we should never go through a day without seeking him. The scriptures also say we should seek the Lord and his strength. The key to all this is to have self-control, which is one of the fruits of the spirit. How do we have self-control? We must think before we act and speak. Slowing down our minds is also a key factor. What does it mean to slow down our minds? We must stop the anxiety, stop thinking about the way things are, and start thinking thoughts of peace. We must put off stress and anxiety and put on peace, rest, and grace. The scriptures tell us to put off the old self and put on the new. That is what the scriptures are talking about. Learning to think differently is key and power.

The only way to hear God is by listening. I didn't say hear. We can hear all day long and never listen. Listening is conductive to actions. This may not work very well at first, but don't give up. Every time we do this, his word writes on our hearts.

Paul says we are letters written on by the spirit of God (2 Corinthians 3:3). We must allow him to write on our hearts. The scriptures say to bring every thought under the obedience of the anointed one our Messiah (2 Corinthians 10:5). There are strongholds in our lives when we are out of control. We must pull down imaginations, and anything that exalts itself before the knowledge of God. We must bring our thoughts captive. If you have ever seen someone being arrested, capturing our thoughts works the same way.

I remember when I first started following the Lord. When I would start praying, vivid pornographic images would come into my mind. I would cry and ask God for forgiveness. Then, when I would pray, the thoughts would come right back. One night, I decided not to allow those thoughts. I took them captive. I looked right at them and said, "You do not have dominion over me. I am a child of God." The thoughts became like broken pixels and faded away. This is learning how the spirit of God works. These things don't always work right away. You must continue doing this until you have the thoughts captive and have self-control. As Paul wrote to the Philippians, "Do not be anxious about anything, but in every situation, by prayer and petition, with thanksgiving, present your requests to God" (Philippians 4:6). Then you will begin experiencing the peace of God that passes all understanding. This keeps our hearts and minds at peace.

In order for the spirit of God to be at its fullest in us, we must allow the proper thoughts on a continual basis. Whatever things are honest, just, pure, lovely, and of good report, we must think on these things. I have been doing this my whole adult life. It doesn't matter how long it takes to overcome something. Don't quit. Don't give up.

What someone focuses on is what he or she becomes. As a person thinks in his or her heart, so he or she is. What someone meditates on the most is what he or she is. What a person allows is what establishes the boundaries in his or her heart, good or bad. We want to make sure the boundaries of our hearts allow the things of God and shut out the world.

We are still talking about how the spirit of God works. It has everything to do with what we allow to go on in our thoughts. What we meditate on the most is written on our hearts. Meditations and emotion write on our hearts. Let us not forget.

How does God work in our prayer lives? Will God answer every prayer we pray? I once knew a lady who ask me to pray for this man to be her husband. The thing was he was married to another woman, and happily at that. I told her I would not and could not. When we pray, we cannot pray in order to consume something with our lust. This is especially true if we are looking to break the commandments of God.

This lady was going to break the God's commands. She was coveting another woman's husband. Second, she was committing adultery in her heart. The scripture say if someone looks upon another person with lust, that person has committed adultery in his or her heart. What we meditate on is what we do or become. When we pray, we must remember to pray according to God's word. We must worship in spirit and in truth.

Why do our prayers remain answered? Is it because of our good works? The only way our prayers are answered is because of our messiah, the son of the living God Jesus/Yeshua. When we have all things that pertain to life and godliness, we know God has answered our prayers. He recognizes his covenant with Jesus and the fact that we are in him. Then he answers our prayers according to his word.

Our biggest problem is in following the Lord but not knowing how he really works. We think because God answers our prayers because he approves of our lifestyles. We think we are faithfully following God. I don't know how many times in my life I have changed my beliefs. I thought all along I was doing what God wanted me to do. I remembered he had been answering my prayers. I felt his presence walking with me as I journeyed along the path. I was teaching errors and not praying properly. I had the wrong belief system. I still had an experience with the Lord and felt his approval. He was walking with me, helping me, and answering my prayers. How do we explain this? How can I get my point across to people who don't understand? The scriptures say to let every person work out his or her own salvation with fear and trembling.

It also says that God works in us to do his will and his good pleasure. God never stops working in us until the day we die. Then, according to the scriptures, his life-giving spirit returns to him. God is going to work in us, and wants us to continue full of fear as we walk along this journey. This is not to be taken lightly at all and it is not my opinion.

Why does God say for us to fear and not to fear? If we are afraid, we have not been made perfect in love. He even says that fear is the beginning of knowledge, but fools despise wisdom and instruction. I would think this is true love. To trust is to listen and obey. This is not what I think; it is what the scriptures teach.

I have heard people say, "What gives you the right to judge me?" It's funny to me that people want to say something like this to uphold the wrong they are doing. God tells us to lie not against the truth, to preach the word in season and out of season, to reprove and rebuke with all long suffering. We don't really have a choice if we are going to obey him.

I love it when people accept what I am saying. It makes me feel better about what I am doing. I would rather offend people than have them lose their lives. The other thing is they will miss out on the plans God has for their lives. I have done that. I wouldn't want to see anyone suffer this loss. We all know it doesn't always feel good to make the right decision. The good thing is it pays for us to choose life.

I know one thing: I become excited when it comes to the things of God. Jeremiah said trying to hold back from telling what God wanted him to say it was like a fire shut up in his bones. I know we have all had that experience, right? If we haven't, we should; it's a life changer. It is important that people hear the truth. The truth saves us from things we would have reaped. That is never fun.

Putting aside the fact that it pleases God, the truth will also fulfill us. This is how the spirit of God works. Do you know why we do things like make bad decisions? We think we will be fulfilled, but we have God-shaped holes inside of us. God is the only one who can fill them. When we are fulfilled, we are complete and whole in this area of our lives.

God really does have what we need. His ways are the right things for us to choose. He made and designed us the way we are, and he tells us what will work according to the design. We are fulfilled according to our designs. God is not just a mean God; he knows we what we do not. We all know this from experience. If we live our lives according to his plan, it will also save those who see us. It is like commercials on TV. When someone does the right thing and another person sees it, the other person follows suit. It comes back around and fulfills the first person. I remember all the times I have repented—truly repented. It feels good. I feel no more shame and no more regret.

A lady once said to me we make things harder on ourselves than God does. The thing that bothered me the most was she didn't realize what she was saying. She was really trying to lead me to give up my peace. She thought, of course, that I was participating in dead works. Repentance is living works. We don't need to go back and lay the foundation of repentance, but we need to always repent when we sin.

When I think of how the Spirit of God works, I think back to 9/11 when those men flew through the twin towers, killing all those people. People began to say that God was judging America. Let's just think about this for a moment. Is God able to put his judgment in the hearts of those men? When we read the scriptures, we see that men are affected.

I am thinking of Pharaoh. The scriptures say his heart was hardened many times by God. The thing is the heart must be able to be hardened. It must also be able to be to be softened. God does not make us choose. He does not mess with free will. He can demand that we make a change and there can be consequences to our choices.

I think we should always look at influence. People can be influenced to do good or bad things. God is not involved in evil; he would only be involved in righteousness. He would also be involved in righteous judgment. What is the righteous judgment of God? It is judgment in tune with no more and no less than what God has told us to follow.

God can't break his own laws. If he did, he would stop being God. All things would fall apart if he stopped being God. There would be nothing but chaos. There would be no rule of order, and lawlessness would take over. Soon, nothing would be left. All would be consumed by lust, and lust turned into nothing. God's judgments are true and righteous.

I hope we are beginning to understand how the Spirit of God works. God is not confused and he is not the author of confusion. He does things in the order he himself established. This is one of the reasons we call him good. He never changes, and he is always the same. That means he is faithful, and we can trust that. He said he is faithful even when we are not. Amen!

I am excited about telling people about who God is and how God works. If we understand how he works, we can follow him and trust him with our whole hearts. God knows this and wants that for us. He also knows it's hard. We live in an evil world. Think of all the lies we hear every day about God and about his word. He says we should prove him and see that he is good.

God has never been out to get us. He has been out to help the ones who want his help. Why did God treat the Jewish people differently than the believers of today? Many people say he was mean to the Jews. This is not true at all. First, there was a whole different covenant with the Jews than with Jesus. The scripture says so.

Some would ask if God is the same and never changes, how is he different? There are several reasons why, but I will only mention a few. He said he would make a new covenant and write his laws on our hearts and in our minds. He also said he would give us soft hearts to be able to receive that new covenant.

The Jews had to follow the laws of God under penalty of death. The law only calls for judgment that had to be paid with a person's life. We are not under the law; we are under grace. Jesus brought grace and truth. Grace fills us with the power to follow the truth and obey it. The scripture says that the love of God has been poured out in our hearts by his spirit. This is also evident in what Jesus did for us and how his spirit pours love into our hearts. When we realize what Jesus has done for us, it fills us with the love of God.

I am glad we could go over some of the ways the spirit of God works. If we don't realize how God does things, we can't follow him very well. He wants us to know how to follow him or he wouldn't have told us to seek him. We should be seeking him in all his ways and learn to be like him. He is our creator; he designed us. We should know our creator as our father. We should also know how much he loves us so we can trust him.

Don't ever forget he is good. We should remind ourselves every day. We should always be thankful for the many blessings he has given us. Seek his face as a flint. Make the sparks fly with your face right up to him.

10

THE EXPLANATION OF THE SPIRIT OF GOD

HERE WE ARE AT THE LAST CHAPTER. I WILL DO MY BEST TO END BY helping us understand what I have said in this book. My hope and desire are that you can teach from this book. Please follow the scripture references. They are at the end of the book. I pray that God helps you receive understanding that you can use.

When I started on this journey, I was not very knowledgeable about the spirit of God. I was only nineteen when I accepted God's call on my life. I grew up in church, which made this journey easier for me. I had some real struggles understanding because of all the belief systems I had to choose from. We all must work through our belief systems. Sometimes we don't even know what a belief system is.

We need to be spiritual people, judge all things, and work through all these belief systems. God's spirit is helping us work through these things. That is the purpose of this book: to help. I pray it does because at the end it will be the same as it was in the days of Noah. People's thoughts in their hearts were evil continually. God said his spirit would not always strive with people because people are also flesh. We must know how God's spirit works so we can judge properly through this mess.

It is hard enough dealing with evil desires—at least it is for me. I don't ever want to take anything for granted in this walk I am on, and I pray you will not either. Growing up, we are taught many things that hinder us later in our lives. We must see things through the eyes of God and pray without stopping.

This is not hopeless at all; there is much hope no matter where we are in our understanding. God knows this. He knew who you were going to be before you were born. David said that we cannot go anywhere without God being there, even in the grave where the dead know nothing. This book is to help you judge through all things with the spirit of God.

The scriptures say that the heart is evil above all else. Who can know it? Learning how to change our hearts would be impossible without God's spirit working with us. God helps soften our hearts by constantly showing us his love for us. We wonder sometimes how God can love us. We fall short so many times. The good thing is God doesn't look at us; he only sees Jesus. This is good for us. This gives us time to grow and break those bondages. I know I have had a few.

When we make decisions, we should judge with spiritual judgment. What is spiritual judgment? It is when we are using God's knowledge and wisdom. It makes more sense to me to use what is going to bring fulfillment. Nothing else will ever fulfill us. We can search, but fulfillment is not going to happen.

When a person judges all things, he or she must use the judgment of God in all things. How we think is very important. The reason is that we could be using our own judgment. Of course, what do I mean by using our own judgment? It means how we have been trained by life and influenced by other people we look up to. We are influenced by our parents, friends, and families. Whatever the influence may be, they could be wrong and misinformed. We must get into our minds and hearts how we should believe and think or meditate. Meditating is key in writing in our hearts how to believe and think. This will ensure that we only have the principles and ways of God to guide us. This also brings with it the life of God manifesting itself.

This is the light that comes to those who follow our lives on a daily basis. This makes all the difference if we want to be the right influence. I would never want to be the wrong influence in someone's life. You ask how can we know? We should only use the Bible to study, and diagram each word during our study. I learned how to interpret scripture in the proper manner. I am talking to the really serious people here, not those who only want to gratify themselves.

I totally believe if you have made it this far, you are one of the serious ones. We should always want to invest in ourselves, especially when it comes to others we want to influence. I love and care about people from all walks of life. Everyone is different in the way he or she hears and communicates. We must remember to be patient with everyone who is serious about change in his or her journey of life.

I would like to talk about the kingdom of God for a moment. Life is what it is, and the rules are very important. Rules are very important because we want to behave rightly and follow rightly as well. The kingdom of God is a government controlled by the judgments of God. Why should God get to call all the shots? Well, he built the world and us, so I am sure he knows what works. He is the designer and head CEO of all things.

God really does know best! He asks us to come, taste, and see that he is good. He has never asked us to take his word for something. That is what people teach us, though, and they believe it. They are very sincere in what they are doing. You can be sincere and totally believe you are right but not be following God.

We need to understand the importance of doing things properly when operating under the government of God. In the kingdom and government of God, we must understand the grave importance of his ways. I know that it is a mercy thing when it comes to doctrines. However,

Paul says we must have biblical doctrines. Of course, a biblical doctrine is a doctrine that agrees with everything from the beginning to the end of the scriptures.

When we think of operating in the kingdom of God, there must be a king, and that king has all authority. We must submit to that rule of authority. He has also placed people inside the government. There is a rule in the church and in the world. Both operate from a different standpoint. The rules are cut and dried in the church. We are the light of the world. The world where God rules is different. God works with what he has. He can use a leader who practices godly principles in ruling the world.

America and Britain have been used by God to rule the world. He has used others to bring judgment or rule to the earth. It would be very hard to see we are not in tune with the God and Father of us all. I have noticed God working in the world all my life. The first time was in my baby bed. It was when Israel won the Six-Day War in June 1967. God also uses and has used Israel to bring light to the world.

God does a lot to bring glory to his name. He always keeps his word and that brings light to the world. If he says something will come to pass, it does. When it does, it lets people see God working. God working brings life and faith to the believer and the nonbeliever. God says in his word to seize every opportunity.

I now want to talk about the life of God. It is the breath of life. It has wisdom, happiness, joy, gladness, faithfulness, self-control, peace, rest, and so on. I think we might be getting the point. When God made people, he put his spirit inside of them and with it came God himself. His spirit gives us life to live. The scriptures say that by him we live, move, and have our beings. I think that covers it well. That is true for the sinner and the born-again believer. How would the lost person ever find God if the spirit of God wasn't in him or her?

How would the spirit of God reprove the world if there were no witnesses? This is hard to understand when people have been trained their whole lives that God is not in the sinner.

They may not be experiencing the fullness of the blessings of God. They are in lost and dying states without the born-again experience. They also don't have the full experience. We know without being born again, there is no way to God in fellowship. We can go to the throne of God as the born-again believer. That is not possible without being born again.

The lost person still has life because of God's spirit. He or she still has the wisdom of God and the principles with which to function. I know before I say this it seems really weird. Even a murderer can walk in the principles of God, and they will work. We define a godly person as someone who walks in God's principles. It changes things quite a bit when we look in the light of truth.

The life of God for the believer is the way we want to experience God. We do not want to experience him as unbelievers. They don't have fellowship with the father. They will not understand from a father God standpoint. The life of God in us will act as death. It will be as a thief that comes to kill, still, and destroy. Why is that? Because there is no love without God. Some people think love is a lot of things it is not. It's not just a good feeling.

Love can hurt quite a bit when you love God and stand up for what is right but everyone around you hates you for it. Love draws us to God and to people. The reason is God is love and defines the rules of love for us in the scriptures. It is not love when we break the commands of God or follow the abominations that God defines in the scriptures. Abominations are things that God hates and plainly tells us not to do.

If we want the fullness of the spirit of God, we must be born again. Then we can be filled with the spirit and understanding. It won't come from dead works, which God does not accept. He says we must come to him and believe he is. He rewards those who diligently seek him. Believing in him is one thing, but believing he rewards those who seek him is totally a different matter.

I totally believe he rewards those who seek him. This all comes from being given a conscience that has the fear of God in it. Paul says the spirit of God and the conscience must work together. Paul also says we can't void the conscience. We can't go against it because it is part of the heart. We must allow our hearts to be influenced and written on so we can begin to experience what God has in mind.

We must know what God says will come to pass. The scriptures say God is not mocked because whatever a person sows he or she will also reap. We must be afraid, knowing that we will reap what we sow. I heard a preacher teaching one week. He said we can pray for crop failure. According to God, we cannot because God is not mocked. We should allow ourselves to become aware of this fact. It would keep us from long lives of suffering.

We would all like to run away from what we have done, but we cannot. We must face the things we have done wrong. The scriptures say we should commit to him even to our own hurt. It is not always going to feel good. We must face the wrongs we have done that bring true repentance. It brings a sorrow that makes us not ashamed to tell anyone what we have done.

As a matter of fact, it brings freedom to us and anyone involved. When I have repented of things, it has been so freeing. I no longer am held back from the true experience God offers me. Praise his name! He is worthy and this proves it. I urge anyone needing to repent to taste the goodness of God. He is waiting on us; let us run to him with outstretched arms. Let him heal us from the inside out. You will not believe how that feels.

I want to bring up something else. I have a question and answers to the question. What is the anointing? We have one on the inside of us. If we are called to the ministry, we have one on us to do the work of the father. The anointing works from the hearts inside of us. When we think of grace, we sometimes don't see the truth. We have been taught that grace is unmerited favor. It is, but it is so much more.

Grace has in it the power of God working from the heart to cause one to be able to do all that a believer must do. It empowers us and does not weigh us down. The commands of God are not grievous to us. They have the spirit of God working in us. Jesus said come unto me all you who labor and are heavy laden and I will give you rest.

As I have said many times, God is a good God. God is good all the time.

Sometimes people see the spirit of God the wrong way. How do people see the spirit of God? I could talk about so many things, but I will only bring up a few. We have learned to see the spirit of God work. This is how we gauge everything we do.

We relate to God the way we see him. Do we see him as a good God? What does it mean to see him as good? If we look at how we relate to that from what we have learned, we will miss how he works altogether. We must remember that he is love and we must remember there are rules for this love.

How we see the spirit of God is how we relate to him. If you take a prism and shine pure light through it, the light comes out in different colors. The prism bends the light. This is what we see in today's society. With the rainbow colors, they say it is true love when we accept people for who they are. People are just different colors. These things they promote are abominations to God, so is that really love? I would say not; we must be aware and awake.

Being awake and aware of what is really going on will save people from perishing. By perishing, I mean embracing chaos, lawlessness, and the spirit of iniquity. Most people haven't recognized the truth about the lawless one. They have been taught it is only one man. People stop gauging anything when they refuse the correction of the Lord.

The Lord does correct and discipline, and sometimes it is not fun. We can trust him; he is faithful. He has proven himself through thousands of years of never leaving us. He has worked with kings, prophets, judges, priests, women, and children. He has spoken to us through his son in the death, burial, and resurrection and also in the things he taught.

The scriptures are here to teach us all things as the spirit of God leads us. Without Jesus's death, burial, and resurrection and our faith in him as the son of God, we cannot experience salvation at the born-again level. We talked about this earlier. Unless we understand this, we miss out on how the spirit of God works in the believer. Everything must be filtered through the salvation we have in Jesus.

If we come to the Lord other than through Jesus, we will not get what we seek. In our names or any one else's, we can't stand for what Jesus has done. No one has lived out his or her life without breaking the commands of God. The law requires death as the payment. Jesus did both; he lived out the law without breaking it. He also died for us so we would not have to die. We could not pay for ourselves; it had to be Jesus. Our names stand for who we are and what we are (Revelation 5:1–14)

BIBLIOGRAPHY

Anderson, Stephen R. "How many languages are there in the world?" Linguistic Society of America. Accessed January 5, 2024. https://www. linguisticsociety.org/content/how-many-languages-are-there-world.

Gesenius, H.W.F. *Hebrew and Chaldee Lexicon to the Old Testament Scriptures*. Grand Rapids, MI: Baker Publishing Group, 1979.

Kobliner, Beth. "Money habits are set by age 7. Teach your kids the value of a dollar now." PBS News Hour. Posted April 5, 2018. https://www. pbs.org/newshour/economy/making-sense/money-habits-are-set-by-age-7-teach-your-kids-the-value-of-a-dollar-now.

McEvoy, Colin. "Jeffrey Dahmer." Biography. Last updated September 15, 2023. https://www.biography.com/crime/jeffrey-dahmer#childhood-and-family.

Thayer, Joseph. *Thayer's Greek-English Lexicon of the New Testament*. Peabody, MA: Hendrickson Academic, 2023.

SCRIPTURES

Chapter One

Acts 2:17; Hebrews 8:10 and 10:16; Jeremiah 31:33; John 10:10; Romans 2:15; Hebrews 13:9; 1 Timothy 4:1; Hebrews 4:16; 2 Timothy 2:13; Philippians 4:8; Isaiah 53; 1 John 1:5–10; Luke 18:11; 2 Corinthians 5:21; Romans 5:6; Matthew 6:33–34; John 3:16, 17; Proverbs 13:12, 23:7, and 4:23.

Chapter Two

Genesis 6; 1 Corinthians 2; Romans 24:3; Proverbs 23:7; Matthew 13; Hebrews 4:12; Proverbs 13:12, 12, 18:24, 27:17, and 22:24–25; Colossians 1:16; Hebrews 11; Acts 17:28; Romans 12:1 and 2; Isaiah 35:8; 1 John 2:6; Proverbs 14:12 and 18:21

Chapter Three

Isaiah 9:7; Luke 1:33; Revelation 11:15; Daniel 7:14; Daniel 2:44; Acts 2; Jeremiah 31:31–34; Hebrews 8:8; Isaiah 59:21; Hebrews 10:16–26; Isaiah 9:6; 1 Peter 2:9 and 2:5; Romans 12:1; Hebrews 13:15; Ephesians 5:2; Luke 17:20–21; Galatians 6:7–9; Proverbs 18:21; Luke 8:18 (AMP); Proverbs 23:7; Matthew 5:28; Romans 3:27 (ESV); 1 John 1:3; Genesis 2:15

Chapter Four

Genesis 2:7; Job 33:4; Acts 17:25; Nehemiah 9:6; 1 Timothy 6:13; John 1:3–4 and 10:10; 2 Peter 1:3; John 5:24; Proverbs 4:23 and 1:5–7; John 10:10; Joshua 1:8; Hebrews11:1 and 11:6; Romans 12:2; Psalm

34:8–10; Hebrews 12:11; Galatians 6:7; 2 Peter 1:3; Mark 8:36; Psalm 107:20; Jeremiah 30:19; Hebrews 4:12; Proverbs 18:21; John 3:18–21; Hebrews10:31; Philippians 2:12; Mark 4:23–24 (AMP); Romans12:1–2

Chapter Five

Romans 9:1; Proverbs 22:6; Matthew 13:1–9 and 18–23; Romans 10:10–11, Hebrews 4:12; John 6:63; Luke 5:22; Job 38:4–42:6; John12; 2 Corinthians 5:17–21; Hebrews 4:16; John 3; Romans 2:7; John5:39–44; Luke 8:15; Hebrews 10:16; Jeremiah 31:33; Ezekiel 36:26; Hebrews 8:10; Philippians 2:12; John 4:24; Hebrews 4:12; John 6:63; Acts 20:27; Hebrews 6; Proverbs 2:6–8; Job 38:4–30; Galatians 6:6–7; John 3; Galatians 3:24–25; Philippians 2:12; John 8:30–32

Chapter Six

Genesis 3:1–19; Galatians 6:7–9; Acts 9:18; 2 Timothy2:15; 1 Corinthians 2:9–15; Hebrews 4:16; 2 Corinthians 5:17–21; John 3:16–17; Hebrews 6:4–5; Psalm 34:1–22; 1 Peter 2:2–3; Hebrews 4:12; Mark 7:6–13; 1 Corinthians 13; John 4:24; John 10:10; Philippians 4:11–13; Proverbs 23:7 and 4:23; Matthew 16:25–27; Exodus 20:17–26; Romans13; James 4

Chapter Seven

1 John 2:20; Psalm 133:2; Leviticus 8:12 and 21:12; Exodus 30:30; 1 Samuel 16:1–13; John 14:31, 12:49, 8:42, and17:8; Luke 4:18; 2 Timothy 4:2; 1 Peter 5:2–3; 2 Peter 1:3–4 and 9; Acts 10:38; Luke 24:19; Ephesians 1:11–13; Acts 9; Galatians 1:15–17; Hebrews 13:5–6; John 14:26, 14:16–17, 16:7, and 7:38–39; Acts 2:33; 2 Timothy 3:5–7; Mark 16:20; John 7:38; Luke 14:28–29

Chapter Eight

Ecclesiastes 11:9–10 (MSG); 1 Samuel 55:11; Exodus 7:3, 13, 14, and 22; 1 Corinthians 14:32 and 14; 2 Peter 3:15–16; Acts 2; 1 John 4:1–6; Deuteronomy 18:9–14; Revelation 22:14–15; Acts 16:17; Job 38:4–42:6; 1 Corinthians 13

Chapter Nine

Malachi 3:6–10; Lamentations 3:22; 2 Timothy 2:13; Matthew 24:37–39; Genesis 6; Hebrews13:5–6; Romans 8:28; Zechariah 4:6–8; John 4:24; Psalm 105:4; Galatians 5:22–23; Romans 7:18; Proverbs 25:27–28; 1 Corinthians 7:5; 1 Timothy 3:2–3; Titus 2:11–12; 2 Peter 1:5–8; 2 Timothy 1:7; 1 Corinthians 9:24–25; Ephesians 4:22; 1Corinthians 3:3; Ezekiel 11:19 and 36:26; Jeremiah 31:33; 2 Corinthians 10:5–6; Philippians 4:6–8; Joshua 1:8; Colossians 2:10; 2 Corinthians 5:21; Romans 3:24, 6:11, 8:2, and 12:5; 1 Corinthians 1:2, 4, and 30 and 15:22; 2 Corinthians 1:21; Philippians 2:12; Hebrews 12:11; James. 3:14; Jeremiah 20:9; 1 Corinthians 14:33

Chapter Ten

Psalm 139:7–12; Hebrews 6; Galatians 6:10 and 5:22–23; Acts 17:28; John 10:10; Hebrews 11:6; Romans 9:1; Acts 23:1–5; Psalm 15:4; 1 John5:2–3

Printed in the United States
by Baker & Taylor Publisher Services

Printed in the United States
by Baker & Taylor Publisher Services